Mary Meade's

Magic Recipes

for the

Electric Blender

Mary Meade's

THE BOBBS-MERRILL COMPANY, INC.
Publishers

Magic Recipes

for the

Electric Blender

by RUTH ELLEN CHURCH

A Subsidiary of Howard W. Sams & Co., Inc.

INDIANAPOLIS • KANSAS CITY • NEW YORK

For Morrison Wood

whose enthusiastic review of this book thirteen years ago launched its successful career, with my grateful thanks.

RUTH ELLEN CHURCH
June, 1965

Contents

Contents

Mary Meade's

Magic Recipes

for the

Electric Blender

1

What Is a Blender?

A blender is an electrical appliance that makes daily meal preparation and entertaining less work and more fun. It takes the nuisance and clutter out of chopping, grating, puréeing and mincing; it mixes or whips foods in just a few seconds; and it does something no other appliance can do—liquefies fruits, vegetables and other solid foods, thus making possible an entirely new kind of cooking.

Originally developed as a drink mixer, for turning out exotic frozen daiquiris, fresh pineapple drinks and malted milks, the early blenders were greeted with glee by healthfood fans who found they could now have their daily portions of fresh carrot juice with parsley and green pepper without going to any trouble at all. A blender will reduce even eggshells and apple cores to a liquid state, and some of the first health drinks popularized called for these ingredients.

Most blenders now on the market are basically alike in that they consist of a powerful little motor in an enclosed base, and a covered container of over a quart capacity, which fits upon the base. The container is equipped with four very sharp stainless-steel blades that make thousands of revolutions per minute, cutting the food in fine pieces, pulverizing it or liquefying it, as you wish. Most blenders now have multiple speeds; all are capable of a high-speed whirlwind action, which is slowed to varying degrees by the kind and amount of food put into the container.

1

Most blenders have containers of heat-resistant glass or plastic so that you may put a froth on hot chocolate or cocoa or smooth the texture of a hot soup or sauce. The blender cover is necessary to keep food from splashing over the sides under the terrific force of the steel propeller. Some covers have tops with a removable center cap so that ingredients may be added, without splashing, to a mix in the container while the motor is running.

Blenders vary somewhat in design and construction. It is well for the prospective purchaser to examine several and watch a demonstration of each, if possible, before making a purchase. Most will perform the usual blender jobs neatly, but there are some differences in design that may make one more convenient than another.

Several blenders come apart at the base of the container so that the parts may be washed separately. One machine will operate with small jars screwed into the base as well as with the conventional blender top. This makes it possible for you to prepare sauces, salad dressings and spreads in half-pint jars and to store them in the same jars. These jars are stronger and safer than canning jars, as they are made especially for blender use. (Canning jars will fit this blender but should not be used.)

A metal container is obtainable for another make blender. This is what bartenders use, because it gets so cold. Most homemakers prefer glass so that they can see how well the food is being mixed.

A blender with a heavy base that sits firmly on the counter while it works is preferable to one with a lighter weight base which may allow it to skid around when there is a heavy load in the container. See that the model you buy doesn't tip easily.

Buy a blender you'll enjoy looking at as well as using, for a blender should be out on your kitchen counter, not tucked away in a cupboard. If it is out, you'll use it half a dozen times a day—to blend the breakfast frozen juice, and the pancake mix, to whirl together a soup for lunch, and to prepare a delightful cocktail before dinner, to make the meat sauce, salad dressing and possibly the dessert. Then you can send the children happily to bed with a strawberry milk shake or an eggnog.

What Will a Blender Do?

A blender will liquefy, blend, mix, chop, grate, purée or neatly pulverize food. It will whip cream or make butter.

It will whirl up the finest frothy drinks you've ever drunk, from a raw-carrot-and-fresh-pineapple cocktail to a brandy eggnog.

It will turn your leftovers into smooth, creamy soups and make other soups with fresher flavors than you've ever tasted.

It will chop vegetables as you like them for salad; mince onions without tears; grate fresh coconut for a curry, potatoes for potato pancakes, and orange and lemon rinds.

It will make salad dressings so perfectly emulsified that no trace of the garlic can be found, though the flavor is evident. Watercress or parsley, capers or anchovies, pickles or cheese can be evenly blended into a dressing that won't separate.

It will grate or chop nuts or reduce them to a nut butter. Cashew, pecan, walnut butters are new taste thrills easily made in a blender.

It will make delectable dips and dunks from cheeses, shrimp, ham, chicken, avocados.

It will make perfect, smooth sauces. Gone forever is the lumpy cream sauce, bumpy gravy, the curdled hollandaise.

It will cut crumbs coarse for stuffing, fine for coating chops and making graham-cracker crusts.

It will dissolve gelatin without preliminary soaking.

It will make applesauce with a wholly new, really *fresh* flavor—and you needn't peel the apples.

It will make a sherbet or frappé which you can eat right from the blender, from a mixture of fruit, juice and crushed ice.

It will mix a cake from a prepared mix or from your own favorite recipe in a twinkling. It mixes pancakes, waffles, quick breads, omelets in seconds.

Blenders can be used to prepare baby foods and puréed

foods for special diets. Your doctor's recommendations should be followed, first of all; then follow the directions of the blender manufacturer.

The best of the blenders will grind coffee and spices.

Read the booklet that comes with your blender to see what *your* blender can do!

How to Use a Blender

Always keep at hand a slim rubber spatula. You'll use it not only to scrape out the last of the food in the container, but to keep the food in the path of the blades.

In working with a heavy mixture, the spatula is needed to push ingredients from the sides of the container to the center when the action slows. Keep the spatula out of the blades or you'll have lumps of rubber in the cheese dip!

Liquids ordinarily go into the container first. Usually you need enough liquid to cover blender blades to get things going.

Always put on the cover before starting the motor.

Cut vegetables, meats and other firm foods into pieces not larger than an inch in diameter. Cut cheese into ½-inch cubes for grating. Tear apart bread when you are converting it to coarse or fine crumbs.

Avoid overblending.

Seconds, not minutes, count! If you blend the ham too long, you have paste, not chopped meat. Vegetables are chopped in moments, reduced to liquid in moments more.

Avoid overworking your motor.

Follow manufacturer's directions about the size of the load. Add extra liquid when a mixture is so thick the motor grinds and balks. And stir it up from the bottom, motor off, with that spatula.

Work with Small Amounts

This is extremely important, especially with solids. Too much food will clog the blender blades and prevent them from operating. With liquids, three-fourths full is fine; but a heavier semi-liquid mixture slows the action, and you may not be able to work with more than one-third or one-half capacity. Hot mixtures tend to "boil up," so don't overfill, and use low speed if you can.

Cut or break solids into pieces before adding them to the container. Break crackers or bread in, a few crackers or one slice at a time, blend the crumbs as fine as you want, pour into a bowl and begin over again. Use the same principle with chocolate, coconut, carrots, fruit—anything you want to chop, grate or reduce to fine particles.

When you switch on the blender always place your hand on the cover to avoid the possibility of a splashover and to stabilize the machine for the first impact of the blades against the food to be blended. Always be sure the container is firmly seated on the base before operating.

How to Chop Raw Vegetables

It's easy, working with small amounts and 1-inch pieces. A quick on-and-off technique with the motor sets the vegetables in motion. For large amounts or finer texture, it is easier to add cold water, which may be drained off in a colander when the vegetables are chopped just as you wish them. The liquid in many recipes will be sufficient without any draining.

How to Care for a Blender

Your machine probably won't need oiling. (Consult your booklet to see.) Usually all you need to do is keep it clean and treat it with respect.

Wipe off the base with a damp cloth after using. Put a little detergent and warm water in the top, turn the switch, and your blender will wash itself. Or put container into the dishpan and give it a good sudsing. Always rinse it well and dry it carefully. For cleaning, take apart the kind of container that comes apart. Don't attempt to sterilize the blender. Normal washing and rinsing keeps it clean, even for baby foods. Washing in the electric dishwasher is not recommended. It may dry out the lubrication in the blades.

Keep Your Blender Working

Keep your blender on a counter so that it will always be handy. You'll find it useful every day.

2

Appetizers, Dips, Dunks and Spreads

The chopping, beating and whipping actions of blender blades transform solids into smooth-as-satin mixtures that pile in a bowl to make a cocktail dip, or almost instantly convert them into chopped pieces as fine as you may want for a spread. The blender is your servant: it will swallow up the garlic and the parsley, making them one with the cheese; it will create *pâté de foie gras* for you out of the liver of the Christmas goose; it will transform peanuts, pecans or cashews into nut butter.

In general you'll need about ¼ cup liquid to start your mixing action for dips and spreads. When they should contain chopped ingredients, do the chopping first, at low speed, and fold them in later; or add them at the last, and don't let the blender convert them into fine particles. Green pepper and onion or nuts can be chopped and distributed perfectly in the mix if you add them just a second or two before you turn the motor off.

Use a rubber spatula with thick mixtures to help things along. Move it up and down rapidly tight against sides of container. Work the top of the mixture, but be careful not to get down into the blades with the motor running. You may end with chopped rubber in your dunk, and it really isn't very good. So poke carefully, and shut off the motor to free the blades if they bog down. Sometimes a quick switching on and off will get things started again. At any rate, never use a metal spoon or knife.

7

APPETIZERS OF SUNDRY KINDS

Appetizer Cheese Cake

(12 portions)

The cheese is in the crackers layered with sour cream and fine-cut vegetables.

Crush in blender and set aside cheese crackers to measure

2 cups crushed cheese crackers

Chop separately in blender, then combine in a bowl

1 green pepper, in pieces
½ cup sliced celery
1 onion, quartered
½ cup stuffed olives

Stir in

2 cups sour cream
1 teaspoon salt
¼ teaspoon paprika
2 tablespoons lemon juice
1 teaspoon worcestershire sauce
Few drops tabasco sauce

Butter bottom and sides of 8-inch round cake pan. Line with wax paper. Sprinkle about ¼ of the crackers in pan. Add a layer of cream and vegetables. Alternate layers of crumbs and cream mixture, ending with crumbs. Chill at least 24 hours. Turn out onto a plate and cut into wedges to serve. Garnish with greens and whole olives.

Onion Tartlets

(4 servings)

Serve them warm with cocktails.

Line tart shells with pastry (your own or a mix) and flute rims. Bake 10 minutes at 400°. Meanwhile, in blender container chop onions to make

> 2 cups chopped onions

Empty into pastry shells, dividing evenly. In blender container place

> 2 eggs
> 1 cup sour cream
> 6 strips bacon, cooked crisp and crumbled
> ¾ teaspoon salt

Blend a few seconds and pour into tart shells. Stir lightly to distribute onions in the custard. Bake tarts and filling at 350° for 15 minutes or until custard is set. Sprinkle tops of pies with

> Minced chives

Serve at once or while still warm.

Sauerkraut Balls

(Appetizers for 8)

They'll be the hit of the party and may be frozen ahead.

Blender-chop, then sauté in 3 tablespoons butter

> 1 onion, quartered
> 5 sprigs parsley

In blender container place

> ½ cup bouillon
> 1 pound (about 2 cups) sauerkraut, drained
> 2 cups diced cooked ham or corned beef

Blend until fine. Add to onion and parsley and cook gently. Sprinkle with

> ⅓ cup flour

Cook and stir until thick. Spread in pan to cool. Shape balls, 1 inch in diameter, and roll in

1 cup fine dry blender-made crumbs

Fry until golden brown in deep fat, heated to 365°. If you make these ahead, and freeze, allow to thaw for 1 hour before frying. Or fry the balls, freeze, and reheat in the oven at 350°.

Quiche Lorraine

(12 appetizer servings; 6 as entree)

American hostesses have adopted this French delight. Serve it with champagne at the beginning of a dinner party.

In a 9-inch unbaked pie shell overlap

> 12 slices pre-cooked (not crisp) bacon, cut in half
> 12 thin slices Swiss cheese, width of bacon

In blender container place

> 4 eggs
> 1 tablespoon flour
> ¾ teaspoon salt
> Few grains pepper
> Dash nutmeg
> 2 cups light cream
> 1 tablespoon soft butter
> 1 slice onion or 4 green onions with tops, sliced

Blend this mixture smooth and pour into lined pie shell. Bake at 375° about 40 minutes, or until set. Serve warm.

Shrimps Remoulade

(8 to 10 servings)

Accompany with cocktail picks, or serve on lettuce as a first course.

Whirl in blender until emulsified

> 1¼ cups olive oil
> ½ cup prepared mustard (Dijon type)

⅓ cup wine vinegar
1½ teaspoons salt
1 small clove garlic
½ teaspoon tabasco sauce
2 tablespoons paprika

Add gradually and blend until chopped

1 cup cut celery
¼ cup packed parsley sprigs
½ green pepper, in pieces
6 green onions, cut in inch lengths
1 hard-cooked egg, quartered

Pour over and chill

3 pounds cooked, cleaned and shelled shrimps.

THE DIPS AND DUNKS, MOSTLY CHEESE

The cheese bowl is almost a necessity of modern entertaining. Any and all kinds of cheese convert to dips and spreads very neatly. Very soft mixtures go into a bowl, to be surrounded with crackers, potato chips, vegetables like crisp cauliflower florets and carrot sticks, all meant for dipping and dunking. Heavier mixtures can be piled in a bowl or molded into an attractive shape, and should be accompanied by a butter knife for spreading on the crackers, rye bread or Melba toast.

Have cheese at room temperature. Make your mixture a day ahead, to let the flavors blend and ripen.

Avocado Cream Cheese Dip

(About 1½ cups)

Pale-green and pretty.

3 tablespoons cream
1 tablespoon lemon juice
2 3-ounce packages cream cheese
1 fully ripe avocado, cut in pieces

Thin slice of medium-sized onion
¼ teaspoon salt
Few drops green coloring

Blend ingredients until smooth, using a rubber spatula to push down the top of the mixture if necessary. If it's slow blending, stop the motor and use the spatula around the blades. The green coloring isn't necessary, but it helps accent the avocado color which otherwise is pretty well paled by the cheese.

Blue Cheese Dip with White Wine or Brandy

(1½ cups plus)

Gourmet's choice!

¼ cup white wine or brandy
½ pound blue cheese (or Roquefort, Gorgonzola), broken up
3-ounce package cream cheese
1 teaspoon worcestershire
Sliver garlic
3 or 4 sprigs parsley

Blend until smooth, using rubber spatula as necessary. You could make this with beer instead of wine. That's good, too— and *different!*

Brie or Camembert with Bacon

(Almost a pint)

One of my favorites.

Cook until crisp, then break into blender

½ pound bacon

Add

¼ cup cream
½ pound cream cheese

Thin slice from small onion
3 sections Brie or Camembert
1 tablespoon lemon juice
Dash cayenne pepper

Blend until smooth. This has a satiny texture and wonderful flavor. Use fully ripened Brie or Camembert (soft).

Clam and Cheese Dip

(Around 1½ cups)

A real palate pleaser.

7-ounce can clams with ¼ cup of their liquor
2 3-ounce packages cream cheese
2 teaspoons cut chives or green-onion tops
¼ teaspoon salt
1 teaspoon worcestershire
3 drops tabasco sauce
1 tablespoon lemon juice
4 or 5 sprigs parsley

Blend until smooth, using spatula as necessary.

Cottage Cheese and Caviar Dip

(About 2 cups)

Red caviar is less expensive than the "real" thing; this dip is sufficiently mouth-watering, however.

Whirl smooth in blender

1 pound carton cottage cheese
1 slice mild onion
¼ cup sour cream

Fold in contents of

1 jar red caviar (any size)

Serve chilled with melba toast or use as dip for celery sticks, cauliflower, potato chips and such.

Cottage and Blue Cheese Dip

(About 1½ cups)

Thin it for a delicious dressing for salad.

> 1 cup cottage cheese
> ¼ pound blue cheese, crumbled
> 1 thin slice medium-sized onion
> Dash each: worcestershire, tabasco
> Tiny sliver garlic
> ¼ cup sour cream

Beat until very smooth. Everybody, just everybody, likes this one!

Cottage Cheese and Shrimp Dip

(1¾ cups)

Accompany this one with celery and carrot sticks.

> ¼ cup cream or milk
> ½ pound fresh cooked shrimps or 5-ounce can
> 8 ounces cottage cheese (1 cup)
> 3 tablespoons chili sauce
> 1 teaspoon freeze-dried chives
> 1 tablespoon lemon juice
> Dash worcestershire
> ½ teaspoon salt

Blend to very smooth mixture, using rubber spatula as necessary.

Tri-Cheese Spread with Almonds

(About 2 cups)

Crunchy, this one!

Chop at low speed

> ½ cup salted almonds

Turn into bowl.
Place in blender container

>1 cup sour cream
>1 cup crumbled blue cheese
>1 cup diced process Swiss
>½ cup diced sharp process cheddar
>1 tablespoon worcestershire
>1 sliver garlic
>2 teaspoons paprika

Blend smooth, then add to nuts.

Two-Cheese Dunk with Horseradish

(About 1½ cups)

Unusual, and unusually good!

>½ pound cottage cheese
>1 3-ounce package cream cheese
>1 tablespoon fresh-grated horseradish
>½ teaspoon paprika
>½ teaspoon dry mustard
>About 5 or 6 sprigs parsley
>½ teaspoon poultry seasoning
>½ teaspoon salt

Blend thoroughly. Nobody'll be able to guess what the seasoning is. Use all cottage cheese, if you wish.

Crabmeat Dip

(Nearly 2 cups)

Lobster, shrimp or clams could be substituted in this delicious blend.

Blend smooth in blender container

>¼ cup cream
>¼ cup lemon juice
>2 tablespoons mayonnaise

2 or 3 sliced green onions, with tops
½ teaspoon salt
1 teaspoon worcestershire sauce
Dash tabasco sauce
8 ounces cream cheese

Add and blend smooth

1 can (about 1 cup) crabmeat, all cartilage removed

Serve as dip for crisp raw vegetables, such as green pepper strips, radishes, celery, broccoli or cauliflower buds. Good also on squares of pumpernickel. (A friend of mine adds horseradish, mustard and tarragon to this mixture and says it's even better!)

Cream Cheese and Cheddar Spread

(About 2 cups)

One of the best.

¼ cup cream
¼ cup piccalilli
½ teaspoon salt
½ teaspoon celery salt
1 slice medium-sized onion
1 teaspoon worcestershire
Dash tabasco sauce
½ pound cream cheese
½ pound cheddar, cut in cubes

Whip mixture in the blender until very smooth and creamy, stirring down with rubber spatula occasionally. The success of this spread depends largely on the cheddar—use the sharpest you can find. Smoked cheddar is good.

Deviled Ham and Cheese Spread with Sherry

(About 1½ cups)

Piquant, this!

¼ cup sherry
½ pound cream cheese
1 3-ounce can deviled ham
2 tablespoons drained sweet-pickle relish
1 slice medium-sized onion
1 teaspoon worcestershire
¼ teaspoon dry mustard
¼ teaspoon salt
Dash garlic powder or thin sliver garlic

Blend ingredients until very smooth, using spatula as necessary.

Green Dunk (Watercress)

(Around 2 cups)

Very attractive to the eye as well as to the palate.

½ pound cream cheese
1 slice small onion
Sliver garlic
1 bunch watercress, washed and dried
3 tablespoons lemon juice
½ teaspoon salt
¼ teaspoon white pepper
1 tablespoon horseradish

Blend until smooth, using spatula now and then at the start. Thin this with sour cream or mayonnaise for a fish sauce or salad dressing. My family loves it on shredded cabbage.

Liverwurst Pâté

(About 1½ cups)

You may want more curry—suit yourself!

½ cup cream
½ pound liver sausage
3 ounces cream cheese

>1 tablespoon worcestershire sauce
>½ teaspoon curry seasoning
>2 tablespoons sherry
>¼ teaspoon salt
>¼ teaspoon coarse black pepper
>¼ teaspoon thyme
>¼ teaspoon marjoram
>2 hard-cooked eggs, quartered

Blend mixture until smooth and serve chilled in a bowl with accompanying crackers. A quartered onion might be included with the other seasonings, if you wish.

Liptauer Cheese

(Over 2 cups)

A continental specialty for your nicest parties.

>½ cup sour cream
>1 pound cream cheese, broken up
>¼ pound softened butter
>1 tablespoon anchovy paste
>2 teaspoons capers
>2 shallots or 1 small onion, quartered
>½ teaspoon salt
>1 tablespoon paprika
>2 teaspoons caraway seeds

Whip to a smooth blend. Mold this mixture in a bowl if you like. It is irresistibly, tantalizingly good.

Pink Dunk

(About 1½ cups)

Shocking pink and startling, but very good!

>½ pound softened cream cheese
>6 pickled baby beets, cut in half
>2 tablespoons pickling liquid
>¼ teaspoon celery salt

1 slice medium-sized onion
Dash tabasco

Blend until smooth and thick. You have to reassure people about this one, for they invariably draw back at first sight of the very pinkness of it, thinking you must have got into the Easter-egg coloring. Tell them quickly it's beets; they'll keep coming back for more! Horseradish is a good addition.

Pistachio Cheese Balls

(3 dozen)

Delicious, fattening morsels!

Blender chop and empty into small bowl

1 cup pistachios

In blender container place

2 tablespoons horseradish
1 sliced dill pickle
2 teaspoons capers
1 green onion with top, cut in inch pieces
½ teaspoon salt
8 ounces cream cheese, softened

Blend until smooth and add

½ cup toasted slivered almonds

Blend a second or two, leaving the nuts in little pieces. Shape mixture into balls, roll in the pistachios, coating thickly, and chill until serving time. Serve on picks.

Port and Cheddar

(1 cup)

Use the sharpest of cheddar; this is good!

¼ cup port wine (or sherry)
2 tablespoons cream

¼ teaspoon paprika
Dash onion salt
½ pound very sharp cheddar, diced

Blend until smooth. This one is nice molded in a small bowl. Maybe you'd better double the recipe.

Sapsago Spread

(Nearly 2 cups)

Sapsago is the clover-flavored, hard green cheese of Switzerland.

Break apart into blender container

1 cone sapsago cheese (about 3 ounces)

Switch motor on and off to grate cheese. Stop motor, add

¾ pound (3 sticks) soft butter
3 tablespoons frozen or fresh chives

Blend to smooth, fluffy spread. It's great on pumpernickel or any dark bread. And it's a conversation encourager.

Sardine and Cheese Spread

(About 1½ cups)

Two cheeses, one fish.

1 can boneless, skinless sardines
¼ pound Roquefort or blue cheese
6 ounces (2 small packages) cream cheese
¼ cup diced green pepper
1 tablespoon chives (or 6 long stems, cut)
1 teaspoon prepared mustard

Use the oil from the sardines as well as the fish. Blend everything until very smooth and creamy, using your spatula at first.

Savory Cheese

(About 1½ cups)

A very popular type.

> 2 tablespoons cream
> 1 tablespoon butter
> ¼ pound any blue mold cheese
> 1 3-ounce package cream cheese
> 1 tablespoon worcestershire
> ¼ teaspoon salt
> ½ teaspoon paprika
> ¼ green pepper, in pieces
> 2 dozen stuffed olives

Blend everything until creamy. You could use olive liquid instead of the cream for a little more pungency—not that you need it!

Tuna Pâté

(About 3½ cups)

A big batch, so you can freeze a carton full.

Place in blender container

> ¼ cup chili sauce
> ¼ cup parsley, packed measure
> 1 small onion, quartered
> 1 package softened cream cheese (8 ounces)
> 1 tablespoon worcestershire sauce
> ½ teaspoon tabasco sauce

Blend until smooth, using spatula as necessary. With motor still running, add in pieces

> 3 cans (7 ounces each) tuna, drained

Blend until smooth, pack in a crock or serving dish and chill. Serve with toast rounds, or pumpernickel.

SOME NON-CHEESE DIPS AND SPREADS

Avocado Dip

(Will please 4 of you)

Doubles as salad dressing.

¼ cup mayonnaise (p. 269)
1 soft ripe avocado, peeled and cut in pieces
1 slice onion
Juice ½ lemon
About ½ teaspoon salt
3 drops tabasco sauce

Blend smooth and let ripen in the refrigerator for an hour.

Guacamole

(About 1½ cups)

Pronounce it hwoc-a-MO-lay.

1 ripe tomato, cut in pieces
2 soft avocados
1 green onion, in pieces
1 teaspoon salt
Fresh-ground black pepper
3 tablespoons lemon juice
2 canned green chili peppers

Blend until smooth. Serve as a dip, or pile on sliced tomatoes for an appetizer. If you'd rather have it blander than the Mexicans like their specialty, skip the chili peppers.

Baked Bean Dip

(About 1½ cups)

Make it hot, if you wish, by adding 2 or 3 hot chili peppers.

Blend to smooth paste

> 1 pound can baked beans
> 1 tablespoon horseradish mustard

Add and blend until chopped

> 1 onion, quartered
> ½ green pepper, cut in pieces
> ½ pound bacon, cooked crisp, crumbled

Dip may be served cold or warmed over candle warmer. Accompany with corn chips.

Corned Beef Pâté

(About 1½ cups)

Take one can of corned beef...

Place in blender container

> ¼ cup red table wine
> ½ cup sour cream
> 1 small onion, quartered
> ½ teaspoon salt
> ½ teaspoon rosemary
> ½ teaspoon monosodium glutamate
> ½ teaspoon dry mustard
> ½ teaspoon tarragon
> 1 tablespoon horseradish
> ¼ teaspoon pepper

Blend until smooth, then add gradually and blend smooth again

> ½ pound (2 cups) fresh mushrooms, sliced
> 1 can (5 ounces) corned beef, cut in dice

Serve chilled with crackers, toast or chips. Provide a knife.

Mary's Good Dunk

(A little more than 1 cup)

Shrimp, celery, carrot and cucumber sticks, radish roses and green onions are good dunkers for this.

1 cup mayonnaise (see p. 269)
½ teaspoon dry mustard
1 tablespoon anchovy paste
½ teaspoon tabasco sauce
2 tablespoons tarragon vinegar
5 sprigs parsley
1 slice onion
1 sliver garlic
3 hard-cooked eggs, quartered

Blend to a smooth sauce and serve cold.

Smoked Egg Dip

(About a pint)

This mixture keeps well and has tantalizing flavor.

½ cup mayonnaise (see p. 269)
¾ teaspoon liquid smoke seasoning
½ teaspoon salt
1 tablespoon soft butter
1 tablespoon lemon juice or vinegar
1 teaspoon prepared mustard
¼ teaspoon black pepper
1 teaspoon worcestershire sauce
Drop or 2 tabasco sauce
6 hard-cooked eggs, quartered

Drop in the eggs gradually with the motor running after you've blended everything else a few moments. Use the rubber spatula as necessary. This smooth mixture not only is good as a dip, but makes an excellent topper for a sliced tomato salad.

Deviled Ham Dip

(Double this amount for more than 6)

Good in sandwiches, too.

> 2 3-ounce cans deviled ham
> 2 hard-cooked eggs, in pieces
> 1 teaspoon horseradish
> 2 tablespoons diced pickle (or thereabouts)
> 1 tablespoon milk

Blend smooth and serve with corn chips, for a change.

Pâté de Foie Gras (or a Reasonable Facsimile)

(About 1½ cups)

This foie is not so gras, being from chicken, not goose.

Sauté

> ½ pound chicken livers in
> ¼ pound butter with
> 1 slice onion

Place in blender with

> ¼ pound (1 cup) fresh mushrooms, raw
> ¼ cup sherry wine
> 1 teaspoon salt
> Dash pepper

Blend everything together until smooth. Pack in a mold and chill. You can use calf's liver either sautéed or simmered, plus melted butter and the other ingredients. That's good, too. Ps-st! You can steal some of the baby's canned chopped liver for a paste like this. Makes it even easier.

Chicken Liver Pâté in Sherry Aspic

(1 quart mold)

To be served with champagne before dinner.

PÂTÉ:

Simmer in water to cover, 5 to 10 minutes, then drain

> 1 pound chicken livers

Place in blender container with the following, and blend smooth

> ½ cup soft butter
> 2 tablespoons lemon juice
> 4 medium onions, cut in pieces
> 2 teaspoons salt
> ¼ teaspoon pepper
> 4 hard-cooked eggs, quartered

ASPIC:

Place in blender container

> 1 tablespoon unflavored gelatin
> ½ cup hot consommé

Blend until gelatin is dissolved. Add

> Remainder of 10½-ounce can consommé (room
>   temperature)
> 1 teaspoon worcestershire sauce
> ½ cup sherry
> ½ teaspoon soy sauce

Switch on the motor for a few seconds, then pour a little of the aspic into the salad mold, turning mold to coat it well. Chill until slightly thickened, then decorate top of mold with

> Slices of hard-cooked egg
> Strips of pimiento
> Slices of stuffed olive

Add remainder of aspic, also thickened. Chill until gelatin begins to set, then add liver pâté. Chill until firm. Turn out pâté with its aspic topping onto a platter and garnish with greens for serving. Accompany with crackers.

Shrimp Pâté

(About 2 cups)

Serve it with wine before dinner.

Place in blender container

> ¼ cup white table wine or sherry
> 1½ tablespoons lemon juice
> ¼ pound (1 stick) butter, softened
> 2 teaspoons Dijon mustard
> ½ teaspoon salt
> ¼ teaspoon mace
> 2 or 3 drops tabasco sauce

Blend smooth, then add a few at a time and blend until chopped

> 1 pound cooked shelled shrimps

Serve with thin slices of toasted French bread.

Tarama (Carp Roe) Spread

(About 1½ cups)

A Greek delicacy, inexpensive and tasty.

Place in blender container and blend smooth

> 5 ounces carp roe

Add gradually, with motor running

> 1 cup olive oil

When you have a smooth emulsion, add gradually

> ¼ cup lemon juice

Blend until thick. Add and blend until chopped

  1 medium onion, quartered

Chill spread and serve with toast squares or rye rounds.

Turkey Dip

(About 2 cups)

Remember this savory mixture when you have leftover turkey!

  ¼ cup sherry
  1 carton (16 ounces) dry cottage cheese
  ¼ cup mayonnaise (p. 269)
  ½ teaspoon salt (more if needed)
  2 cups diced cooked turkey
  2 tablespoons fresh or frozen chives

Blend to smooth mixture, using rubber spatula as necessary. Pile in a bowl and sprinkle with more chives as garnish, if you wish.

SPREADS FOR BREADS

There are thousands of these that you can make beautifully in a blender, I'm sure, and many combinations will occur to you after you've tried a few. The blender grinds nuts, chops carrots, minces ham for spreads. Work with small amounts, and use the rubber spatula as you need to, with the motor off, so that you can get down into the blades.

All of the preceding dips and dunks qualify as sandwich spreads, too.

REMEMBER: You can make your own delicious butter simply by over-whipping heavy cream in your blender!

Almond, Cheese and Marmalade Spread

(More than a cupful)

Ladies' choice.

1 3-ounce package cream cheese, cut in pieces
½ cup orange marmalade
¼ cup salted almonds

Have cheese at room temperature. Blend until almonds are chopped fairly fine. If you need liquid to help things along, make it orange juice. This one is nice for rolled tea-party sandwiches.

Apricot Nut Spread

(About 1 cup)

For dainty sandwiches.

1 cup well-drained soaked dried apricots
¼ cup walnuts
¼ cup mayonnaise (p. 269)

Blend, leaving nuts chopped, not minced. You can use the big, soft apricots without soaking. They needn't be completely softened.

Carrot Sandwich Spread

(Makes 4 sandwiches)

A general favorite.

Chop at low speed

2 large carrots, cut in pieces

Turn out and then chop

½ cup salted peanuts

Mix carrots and nuts with

¼ cup mayonnaise (p. 269)

Coarse-cut cabbage and some diced celery can be added with a little more dressing to make a crunchy variation.

Chicken and Roquefort Spread

(About 1¼ cups)

Use this for party sandwiches, the dainty kind.

> ½ cup mayonnaise (p. 269)
> 3 ounces Roquefort cheese, broken up
> ½ teaspoon salt
> 2 cups diced cooked chicken or turkey

Blend mixture to smooth spread, using spatula as necessary.

Chicken, Turkey or Ham Salad Spread

(Enough for 6 sandwiches)

Best when broiled.

> ⅓ cup mayonnaise or other dressing
> 1 cup diced chicken, turkey or ham
> 1 cup diced celery
> 1 tablespoon sweet-pickle relish or 1 small pickle
> Salt, pepper

Blend until finely chopped, using rubber spatula for even mincing with motor off, of course. For something delicious spread this on split buns, top with cheese and broil. Variation: Omit pickle. Add 1 cup pecans and blend only until chopped.

Dried Beef Spread

(About 1½ cups)

Good on whole wheat.

> 2 ounces dried beef or smoked sliced beef
> ½ cup diced cheddar cheese
> ¾ cup salted peanuts
> 1 hard-cooked egg, quartered

1 pimiento
½ cup mayonnaise or cooked dressing

Blend until well mixed and as fine as you like it.

Dried Beef and Tomato Spread

(For 6 hot sandwiches)

This can be your lunch.

1 can condensed tomato soup
4 ounces dried beef or smoked sliced beef
1 cup diced sharp cheese
1 slice onion

Blend smooth, then either top your bread and broil until hot or heat first and spoon over toasted bread. This is even good cold.

Egg and Cheese Spread

(More than a cupful)

A sandwich and soup equals lunch.

2 tablespoons cream
½ cup mayonnaise (p. 269)
¼ pound process pimiento cheese, diced
4 hard-cooked eggs, quartered
1 slice green pepper
Salt, pepper

Blend until well mixed, but leave green pepper in discernible pieces.

Fruit Nut Spread

(For 6 sandwiches)

Teatime treat.

½ cup orange juice
1 tablespoon lemon juice

1 apple, cored, in pieces
1 cup raisins
1 cup walnuts
Dash salt

Blend until mixture is a spreadable paste.

Garden Fresh Spread

(A little over a cupful)

Nice on fresh white bread.

¼ cup Basic French Dressing (page 255)
¼ pound sharp cheese, cubed
½ cucumber, in pieces
1 carrot, sliced
Salt to taste

Blend until carrots are in fairly fine pieces. A few cubes of crisp cabbage or some cauliflower florets may be added.

Meat Spread

(About 1 cup)

Helps use leftovers.

¼ cup mayonnaise (p. 269)
1 cup sliced roast meat (beef, veal, pork or lamb), cut
   in squares
1 slice onion
1 teaspoon prepared horseradish
¼ cup cut celery
½ teaspoon salt

Blend ingredients until meat is finely minced, using spatula as necessary after stopping motor.

Nut Butter

(About ¾ cup)

So easy and so good. Use high speed for the job.

2 tablespoons salad oil or melted butter (optional)
1½ cups salted peanuts, pecans, almonds or cashews

You can make Nut Butter without salad oil, as nuts furnish their own oil, but it takes longer, requires a lot of stopping and starting of the motor and more use of the rubber spatula. If the nuts aren't salted, add 1 teaspoon salt. You may stop blending when the nuts are very fine, but not quite a paste, if you like, and you may use them that way for casserole toppings, curry accompaniments, dressing for cooked vegetables. Ever taste pecan butter? It's delicious and then some!

Olive, Cheese and Bacon Spread

(For 6 sandwiches)

This is one you'll enjoy.

1 cup stuffed olives
¼ pound process cheese, any kind, cubed
4 strips bacon, cooked crisp

Blend ingredients to smooth spread. Add cream or liquid from olives to facilitate things if mixture is too thick to move.

Orange, Cheese and Pecan Filling

(1¼ cups)

Fine for a wedding reception.

¼ cup orange juice
1 cup pecans

Outer peel of ½ orange, in strips
2 3-ounce packages cream cheese

Blend until well mixed and of fairly fine texture.

Salmon and Ripe Olive Spread

(Enough for 6 sandwiches)

Substantial eating.

¼ cup mayonnaise (p. 269)
1 teaspoon lemon juice
½ cup salmon
1 small carrot, in pieces
¼ cup pitted ripe olives
¼ cup diced celery
Salt

Blend until vegetables are finely chopped; stop motor often and stir down contents. Tip: a rib of celery is almost as good a spatula as a spatula, and you can push it down into the blades!

Sardine Spread

(About ¾ cup)

Try this on Melba toast.

2 tablespoons mayonnaise
1 small tin sardines in mustard or tomato sauce
1 tablespoon lemon juice
1 hard-cooked egg, quartered

Blend to smooth paste.

Shrimp or Lobster Paste

(1 cup)

An excellent canapé cover.

2 tablespoons lemon juice or tarragon vinegar
Salt, onion salt, celery salt
2 tablespoons chili sauce
2 tablespoons mayonnaise
1 small can shrimps (4½ or 5 ounces) or 1 cup
   cooked shrimps or lobster meat

Blend to a fine paste. Capers are also good with the spread
if you have them. A teaspoonful is enough.

Walnut, Green Pepper and Cheese Spread

(Well over a cup)

This can be molded for a party.

¼ cup cream
1 green pepper, diced
½ cup walnuts
½ pound cream cheese, diced
Salt, pepper
Dash worcestershire

Blend, leaving pepper and nuts in fine pieces.

Watercress Butter

(Around a cupful)

Full of vitamins!

½ bunch watercress, washed and dried
½ cup soft butter
1 tablespoon lemon juice
½ teaspoon prepared mustard
Salt

Blend until cress is very fine.

3

Breads, Muffins, Pancakes, Waffles—and a Few Cornbreads

"Quick" breads can be put together so fast in the blender that you'll never believe it if you don't try it. Pancakes, especially, are mixed with lightning speed and entirely in the blender container. You can have them with chopped fruit or grated rind as easily as without. Fruit and nut breads, blender-made, are simple as counting to 10.

Remember to keep your rubber spatula handily by, for stirring down a thick mixture (*with the motor off*) when necessary. Have ingredients at room temperature when possible. Shortening or butter should be soft. I don't think you'll run into any difficulties at all with these carefully selected recipes.

BREADS—The Quick Kind and Several with Yeast

Fresh Apple and Orange Bread

(Loaf 9½ by 5½ inches)

Keeps at least a week.

Sift into a bowl

> 3 cups flour
> 1 teaspoon soda
> 1½ teaspoons baking powder
> 1 teaspoon salt

Place in blender container

>½ cup orange juice
>2 eggs
>½ cup shortening
>1⅓ cups sugar

Blend well, then add

>1½ apples, cored, sliced
>¼ orange, including all of peel

Blend until fruit is chopped fine. Add and blend 15 seconds

>1 cup raisins
>½ cup nuts

Stir into dry ingredients. Bake in greased and floured loaf pan at 350° about 1 hour and 15 minutes.

Banana Bran Bread

(1 loaf)

This is a honey-sweetened bread which keeps well.

Place in blender container

>1 egg
>¼ cup soft butter
>¾ cup honey

Switch on motor and with blender running at slow, slice in

>3 bananas (ripe ones)

Add and blend to chop

>½ cup nuts

Pour contents of blender over this mixture in a large bowl

>1½ cups flour
>2 teaspoons baking powder
>½ teaspoon salt

½ teaspoon soda
¾ cup all-bran cereal

Stir together well but don't overmix. Turn into greased pan.
Bake 1 hour at 350°.

Banana Nut Bread

(Loaf 9½ by 5½ inches)

Tender and rich; almost cakelike.

Sift into a bowl

2 cups flour
1½ teaspoons baking powder
½ teaspoon soda

Place in blender container

2 eggs
½ cup soft shortening
1½ tablespoons sour milk
1 teaspoon lemon juice
3 large bananas
1 cup sugar
¼ teaspoon salt

Blend smooth. Add and blend 15 seconds longer

1 cup nuts

Pour over dry ingredients and stir lightly together. Bake in
greased pan at 350° for 45 minutes or until done.

Butterscotch Nut Bread

(Loaf 9½ by 5½ inches)

Flavorsome and easy to make.

Sift together into a bowl

2 cups flour
1½ teaspoons baking powder

¾ teaspoon soda
¼ teaspoon salt

Place in blender container

1 tablespoon fat
1 cup buttermilk
1 egg
1 cup brown sugar, packed

Blend until smooth. Add and blend 15 seconds

½ cup nuts

Pour blended mixture into dry ingredients; mix only until moistened. Pour into greased loaf pan, bake at 350° for 45 minutes or until done.

Date Nut Bread

(2 loaves)

Drip icing over the tops of the loaves if you wish.

Place in blender container

1¾ cups scalded milk
2 teaspoons salt
1 cup brown sugar
½ cup shortening
1 cup pitted dates
½ cup walnuts

Blend until dates and nuts are chopped. Dissolve

2 packages active dry or compressed yeast in
¼ cup warm water

Add to contents of blender which should be lukewarm, with

2 eggs

Blend just to mix. Pour into bowl with

5 cups flour

Mix to smooth soft dough, adding as you need it another

1 cup flour

Knead until smooth and elastic. Place in greased bowl, cover and let rise until doubled in bulk, about 2 hours. Divide dough into two parts. Shape two loaves and place in greased 9½-by-5½-inch pans. Cover and let rise again until double. Bake at 375° for 50 minutes or until done.

Oatmeal Fruit Bread

(Loaf 9½ by 5½ inches)

You can't stop eating it!

Place in container

¼ cup buttermilk
Rind from ½ orange

Blend to grate rind. Add

1 cup buttermilk
½ cup cooked prunes, pitted
½ cup cooked apricots

Blend again until smooth. Add

1 egg
¼ cup shortening
½ cup brown sugar, packed

Blend a few seconds, then add

¾ cup nuts

Blend 10 to 20 seconds. Sift together into a bowl

2 cups flour
2 teaspoons baking powder
¾ teaspoon soda
1 teaspoon salt

Stir in

>   1 cup rolled oats

Add blended mixture. Mix quickly. Turn into large greased loaf pan and bake in moderate oven, 350°, for 1¼ hours. Cool on rack.

Orange Date Bread

(Loaf 9½ by 5½ inches)

Wonderful flavor from a whole orange.

Sift into mixing bowl

>   2 cups flour
>   1½ teaspoons baking powder
>   ½ teaspoon soda

Place in blender

>   ½ cup hot water
>   ⅔ cup dates

Switch on motor and add gradually

>   1 orange, cut in eighths, seeds removed

Blend until finely cut. Add

>   1 egg
>   2 tablespoons soft butter
>   ¼ teaspoon salt
>   ¾ cup sugar

Blend about 30 seconds, then add

>   ½ cup nuts

Blend 15 seconds and turn into dry ingredients. Stir lightly and turn into greased pan. Bake at 350° for 1 hour.

Orange Tea Bread

(9½-by-5½-inch loaf)

You may prefer to call it cake, as the loaf is sweet. Makes good little sandwiches with cream cheese.

Place in blender container

> Outer rind of 2 large oranges
> ¼ cup sugar
> ⅓ cup water

Blend until rind is fine. Pour into small saucepan and simmer 10 minutes. In blender container place

> ¼ cup soft shortening
> ½ cup sugar
> 1 cup buttermilk
> ½ cup raisins
> ½ teaspoon salt

Blend until raisins are chopped. Pour over this combination which has been sifted into a bowl

> 2 cups flour
> 1 teaspoon soda

Stir well. Add orange mixture (cooled). Mix and bake in greased loaf pan at 350° for 1½ hours.

Peanut Butter Bread

(9½-by-5½-inch loaf)

If you like peanut butter, you'll love this bread!

Place in blender container

> 1 cup milk
> 2 eggs
> ½ cup sugar
> 1 cup peanut butter
> 1 teaspoon salt

Blend a few seconds and stir into mixture of

> 2 cups flour
> 3 teaspoons baking powder

Mix lightly and bake in greased loaf pan at 350° for 50 to 60 minutes.

Casserole Onion Bread

(1 loaf)

Versatile onion soup mix makes a savory bread.

In blender container place

> 1 cup scalded milk
> 3 tablespoons sugar
> 1½ tablespoons butter or margarine
> 1 envelope onion soup mix

Blend a few seconds. Soften

> 2 packages active dry or compressed yeast in
> ¾ cup warm water

Add to blender mixture when it is lukewarm. Mix a few seconds and pour into a bowl containing

> 4 cups flour

Stir and mix very well. Cover bowl, let rise in warm place 45 minutes. Stir down batter, beat vigorously and turn into greased 1½-quart casserole. Let rise again until doubled and bake at 375° for 1 hour.

Vegetable Bread

(Loaf 9½ by 5½ inches)

Specks of carrot and parsley, onion and tomato juice add flavor.

Grate in blender in two portions, emptying into a bowl

> 1½ cups sliced carrots

In blender container place

> ½ cup tomato juice
> 1 slice onion
> ¼ cup fresh parsley (or 2 tablespoons dried parsley flakes)
> 1 egg
> 2 tablespoons oil or soft butter
> 2 tablespoons sugar
> 1½ teaspoons salt

Blend until vegetables are chopped fine. Pour mixture into bowl with carrots. Soften

> 1 package active dry or compressed yeast in
> ¼ cup warm water

Add to bowl with

> 3 cups flour

Mix well and knead in about

> ¾ cup more flour

Knead until smooth and elastic. Round up in bowl, grease, cover and let rise until doubled in a warm place. Shape into a loaf and place in greased pan. Cover and let rise until doubled. Bake 1 hour at 375°.

Vegetable Cheese Bread: Add ½ cup cubed sharp cheddar to tomato juice mixture in second step.

MUFFINS—Not the Ordinary Kind

Banana Surprise Tea Muffins

(16 small ones)

The surprise is jelly.

Sift into mixing bowl

> 1¾ cups flour
> 2 teaspoons baking powder
> ¼ teaspoon soda

Place in blender container

> 1 egg
> ⅓ cup salad oil or melted shortening
> 3 bananas
> ¾ teaspoon salt
> ½ cup sugar

Blend smooth, turn into dry ingredients and stir to mix. Leave lumps. Turn into greased small muffin pans. Top each muffin with

> 1 teaspoon jelly

Bake at 400° about 20 minutes.

Carrot Muffins

(1 dozen)

They're colorful, moist and carroty.

Place in blender container

> 1 cup milk
> 1½ cups sliced carrots
> 2 eggs
> 1 teaspoon salt
> 2 tablespoons oil or melted butter

Blend until carrots are fine. Pour mixture over combination of

> 1½ cups flour
> 2 teaspoons baking powder

Bake in buttered custard cups or muffin pans at 425° for about 25 minutes.

Cinnamon Muffins

(8 medium size)

Spicy and tender.

Sift into bowl

> 1 cup flour
> 1½ teaspoons baking powder

Place in blender container

> 1 egg
> ½ cup milk
> ¼ cup melted or soft shortening
> 1½ teaspoons cinnamon
> ¼ teaspoon salt
> ½ cup brown sugar, packed

Blend smooth. Add

> ½ cup raisins

Blend a few seconds and pour over dry ingredients. Stir lightly and turn into greased muffin pans. Bake 15 to 20 minutes at 375°.

Cranberry Orange Muffins

(A dozen and a half, medium size)

Excellent with a simple salad luncheon.

Sift into bowl

> 2 cups flour
> 3 teaspoons baking powder

Place in blender container

> 1 egg
> 1 cup milk
> 1 cup cranberries

Pared rind of 2 oranges
3 tablespoons soft or melted shortening
⅔ cup sugar
1 teaspoon salt

Blend until cranberries are chopped fine. Pour over dry ingredients and stir just to moisten flour. Spoon into greased muffin pans and bake in 400° oven for 25 minutes.

Date Nut Muffins

(1½ dozen medium size)

An irresistible combination.

Sift together into a bowl

2 cups flour
4 teaspoons baking powder
½ teaspoon salt

Place in blender container

1 cup hot milk
½ cup pitted dates

Let stand about 3 minutes, then blend until dates are chopped. Add

¼ cup soft butter or margarine
1 egg
¼ cup sugar

Blend about 1 minute. Add

¼ cup walnuts

Blend about 15 seconds. Pour into sifted dry ingredients and mix only until dry ingredients are dampened. Spoon into greased muffin pans, filling two-thirds full. Bake in 400° oven 20 to 25 minutes.

Ginger Gems

(2 dozen small ones)

Spicy and nice with a fruit-plate lunch.

Sift into a bowl

> 1¾ cups flour
> 1 teaspoon soda

Place in blender container

> ½ cup water
> 2 teaspoons instant coffee
> ¼ cup soft shortening
> 1 egg
> ½ cup molasses
> ½ cup sugar
> ¼ teaspoon each: salt, nutmeg, ginger, cinnamon

Blend until smooth. Turn into dry ingredients and stir lightly together. Fill greased muffin pans two-thirds full and bake at 375° about 20 minutes.

Giant Cheese Popovers

(Eight)

Eat them as they are, huge empty puffs, with butter, or split and fill them with creamed ham, chicken or seafood.

Place in blender container

> 3 eggs
> 1 cup milk
> 2 tablespoons oil
> ½ teaspoon salt
> 1 teaspoon sugar

2 or 3 sprigs parsley (optional)
¾ cup cubes sharp cheddar cheese

Blend at high speed until parsley and cheese are fine and batter is bubbly. Add

1 cup flour

Mix until thoroughly blended. Pour into 8 deep glass baking cups which have been well buttered and placed in a jelly roll pan. Bake at 400° for 50 to 60 minutes, until popovers are high, crusty and well browned.

Yorkshire Pudding

(4 to 6 servings)

The traditional accompaniment to roast beef.

Whirl in blender until smooth and bubbly

1 cup milk
2 eggs
1 teaspoon salt
1 cup flour

Pour into ½ cup hot beef drippings in an 8-inch-square pan and pop into a hot 400° oven. Bake 25 or 30 minutes. Serve hot.

(*Note:* You don't get too much of a drip from roast beef, so if you like Yorkshire pudding, save drippings from steaks in a freezer container. Or bake the pudding around a pot roast, which you may like even better because of the saturation of good brown gravy.)

Toad-in-the-Hole: This English specialty requires 8 to 10 well-browned sausages in the baking pan, together with ¼ cup sausage drippings. Bake as for Yorkshire pudding, using the same batter.

PANCAKES, FRITTERS AND WAFFLES—See How Easy?

Almond Rice Pancakes

(5 servings)

Tender, and a little crunchy—these are special, perhaps for guests. Serve them with applesauce or preserves.

Place in blender container

> 1¾ cups milk
> 1 egg plus 1 yolk
> 1 cup cooked rice
> ½ cup toasted almonds
> 1 cup flour
> 2 teaspoons baking powder
> 1 tablespoon brown sugar
> ½ teaspoon salt
> 2 tablespoons melted butter or oil

Whirl everything together just until almonds are grated, which takes but a few seconds. Bake on hot, lightly greased griddle, turning once. They may be rolled or stacked.

Apple Fritters

(4 servings)

Use the same coating to make any other fruit fritters you like —plum, strawberry, peach.

In blender container place

> ¾ cup milk
> 1 egg
> 1 tablespoon oil
> 1 tablespoon sugar
> ½ teaspoon salt
> 1 cup flour

Cover and blend a few seconds, using rubber spatula in top of mixture if you need to. Pare, core and slice

> 2 flavorsome apples

Spear slices on a fork and dip into batter. Fry in deep fat heated to 365°, until puffy and brown. Drain on paper toweling. Sprinkle with confectioners' sugar. Serve with sirup or as garnish for meat.

Corn Fritters: Omit sugar (or cut it to 1 teaspoon) and use only ½ cup milk in the batter described. Stir in 1 cup whole-kernel corn, drained. Drop batter by spoonfuls into hot fat and cook until well browned. Drain on paper toweling and serve with applesauce or maple sirup.

Apple Pancakes

(For 4 persons)

An excellent choice for a brunch.

Place in blender container

> 1½ cups milk
> 1 egg
> 2 tablespoons oil
> 1½ cups flour
> 3 tablespoons sugar
> 2 teaspoons baking powder
> ½ teaspoon salt
> ½ teaspoon cinnamon
> 2 apples, cored, diced

Blend a few seconds, until batter is mixed and apples are chopped fine. Pour batter from blender container onto hot, lightly greased griddle. Brown on both sides and serve with sirup, whipped cream or sour cream sprinkled with brown sugar.

Banana Wheat Germ Pancakes

(12 to 16 cakes)

Serve them with sirup or crushed, sweetened strawberries.

Place in blender container

> 2 eggs
> 2 cups milk
> ½ teaspoon salt
> 1 cup flour
> 1 teaspoon baking powder
> ½ cup wheat germ
> ½ banana, sliced

Blend a few seconds and bake pancakes on a hot, lightly greased griddle, turning once.

Cheese Blintzes

(18 to 24 pancakes; 6 servings)

Any leftover filling will be great in an omelet next morning.

Blend a few seconds, until smooth

> 3 eggs
> ¾ cup milk
> ¼ teaspoon salt
> ¾ cup flour

Heat shallow 6- or 7-inch skillet; brush with melted butter. Pour in only enough batter at a time to make a very thin pancake, rotating the pan to spread it evenly to the edges. These cakes should be paper thin. Brown only on the bottom, by which time the top should be dry. Turn out onto a paper towel. Stack all the cakes.

Blend smooth

> 1 egg yolk
> 1 pound dry cottage cheese

¼ cup sugar
¼ teaspoon cinnamon
¼ teaspoon salt

Put a spoonful of filling across the center of each pancake, on the cooked side. Fold in sides over filling, then fold the other way to make neat packages. Fry until brown in butter and serve hot with preserves or fruit. (These delicious delicacies may be prepared ahead and frozen, except for the final butter-browning.)

Chicken Filled Crêpes

(6 servings)

A delectable supper dish, with a touch of wine to flavor it.

Blend and bake

> 1 batch pancakes for Blintzes, preceding page
> (brown both sides)

Sauté

> ½ pound fresh mushrooms in
> ⅓ cup butter

Turn into blender container with

> ⅓ cup flour
> ½ teaspoon salt
> 1 cup cream
> 1 cup chicken broth
> 4 or 5 parsley sprigs

Blend until mushrooms and parsley are chopped. Turn into saucepan and cook until thickened, stirring constantly. Add

> ½ cup dry white wine
> ½ cup grated parmesan cheese

Chop in blender

> 2 cups diced chicken or turkey

Turn into small bowl and add enough of the sauce to moisten chicken. Fill and roll pancakes and place in buttered baking dish, side by side. Pour rest of sauce over them and sprinkle with

½ cup more parmesan cheese

Bake 15 minutes at 375°, or brown until hot under broiler.

Cottage Cheese Pancakes

(4 servings)

Some people like these with butter, cinnamon and sugar.

> 4 eggs
> ⅓ cup light cream
> 1 pound cottage cheese
> 1 teaspoon salt
> 1 cup flour
> 1 teaspoon baking powder

Whirl all ingredients in blender until bubbly, just a few seconds. Pour onto hot lightly greased griddle and bake on both sides, turning once.

Crêpes Suzette

(8 cakes, 2 to a customer)

Spectacular, delicious.

Place in blender container

> 1 cup milk
> 3 eggs
> ⅓ cup sugar
> ¼ cup melted or soft butter
> ¼ teaspoon salt
> 1 piece outer rind of lemon
> ¼ cup orange juice

Blend smooth, and add gradually with motor running

1¾ cups sifted cake flour

When batter is smooth bake one pancake at a time in lightly greased, hot 9-inch skillet, using ¼ cup batter per pancake. Bake until brown on one side, turn and bake the other side. (Cakes may be made ahead of time and reheated with the sauce.) Spread each pancake with Suzette butter. Make this by mixing by hand

> 1¼ cups sifted confectioners' sugar
> ½ cup soft butter
> 1 teaspoon grated orange rind
> 3 tablespoons orange juice

Roll pancakes with filling inside. Place filled pancakes in heated skillet or chafing dish and make a sauce by combining

> ⅓ cup brandy
> ¼ cup curaçao

Add 2 tablespoons sauce to crêpes, heat thoroughly and pour the rest of the sauce over the cakes. Ignite and serve flaming.

Orange Pancakes

(A dozen smallish ones; for 4)

These can be for dessert.

Place in blender container

> Outer rind of ½ orange
> 1 cup orange juice
> ¼ cup milk
> 3 tablespoons melted shortening or salad oil
> 1 egg
> 3 tablespoons sugar
> ¾ teaspoon salt
> 1¼ cups sifted flour
> 2½ teaspoons baking powder

Switch on motor and run 15 seconds. Stop motor, scrape down batter with rubber spatula and blend again until smooth.

You can pour a pancake batter right from the blender to the griddle if you like. Bake these on a lightly greased, hot griddle and serve with Orange Sauce (p. 293).

Potato Pancakes

(10 or 12)

Miraculously easy!

Place in blender

>   3 eggs

Start blender and slice in

>   5 or 6 medium-sized potatoes, pared
>   3 slices onion
>   2 large sprigs parsley

Blend until all vegetables are cut fine. Add

>   ⅓ cup flour
>   ¼ teaspoon baking powder
>   1½ teaspoons salt

Blend just to mix. Fry in bacon drippings in a hot skillet. Serve with Applesauce (page 112) or gooseberry sauce. These are delicious. Gone is the work of grating which used to prevent many a lover of potato pancakes from making them.

Cheese Waffles

(6 large ones)

Nice for lunch.

Sift into bowl

>   2 cups flour
>   3 teaspoons baking powder

Place in blender container

> 3 egg yolks
> 1¼ cups milk
> ¼ cup salad oil or melted fat
> 2 teaspoons sugar
> ½ teaspoon salt
> 1 cup diced sharp cheddar cheese

Blend smooth and pour over dry ingredients; mix lightly. Fold in

> 3 egg whites, beaten stiff

Bake in hot waffle iron. Serve with sirup or as base for creamed chicken.

Pecan Waffles

Use the preceding recipe, but omit cheese and sprinkle each waffle before baking with broken pecans.

Chocolate Waffles

(Eight 7-inchers)

A delightful dessert.

Sift into a bowl

> 2 cups flour
> 3 teaspoons baking powder

Place in blender container

> 3 egg yolks
> ½ cup sugar
> 1 teaspoon salt
> 1½ cups milk
> ¼ cup soft shortening
> 2 ounces unsweetened chocolate, melted
> ½ teaspoon vanilla

Blend thoroughly, pour over flour, stir lightly and fold in

> 3 egg whites, beaten stiff

Bake in hot waffle iron. Serve as dessert with whipped cream.

A FEW CORNBREADS

Chicken Spoon Bread

(6 servings)

It's good with chicken gravy, mushroom sauce, or just butter.

Place in blender container

> 2 cups milk
> 2 tablespoons oil or melted butter
> 1 teaspoon salt
> ½ cup yellow or white cornmeal
> ½ teaspoon baking powder
> 3 egg yolks

Blend a few seconds at high speed. Then turn to low speed and add

> 1 cup diced cooked chicken

Blend just a few seconds to chop chicken, not too fine. Fold into

> 3 egg whites, beaten stiff

Pour into buttered 1½-quart casserole and bake at 375° about 45 minutes or until firm. Serve hot, spooned from the baking dish.

Hush Puppies

(About 1½ dozen)

Fish-fry food in the South, dating from Colonial days.

In blender container put

> 1 cup buttermilk
> 1 egg
> 1 teaspoon salt
> 1 small onion, quartered

Blend until onion is chopped. Pour over mixture of

> 2 cups cornmeal
> 1 teaspoon baking powder
> ½ teaspoon soda
> 1 tablespoon flour

Mix with spoon and drop by teaspoonfuls into deep hot fat, 375°. Fry golden brown.

Waffley Cornbread

(8 servings)

Everything goes into the blender, one, two, three!

> 1 cup milk
> ½ cup cream
> 2 eggs
> 1 teaspoon salt
> ½ cup flour
> 2 tablespoons sugar
> 3 teaspoons baking powder
> 2¼ cups cornmeal

Run spatula to bottom of blender container several times before starting motor. Cover. Switch on motor and run half a minute, or until vortex forms in contents. Use spatula a time or two in upper part of container. Bake waffles to serve with sirup or as base for creamed chicken. Waffles also may be served as bread.

Two or three strips of crisp bacon could be crumbled into the blender for these.

4

Cakes and Cookies

I had to be convinced that good cakes can be made in the electric blender. I used to take the know-it-all attitude that it was impossible to make a cake worth eating that way. Now I know better. Having made hundreds of blended cakes, I know that some cakes adapt to this method better than others, but that it is possible to make dozens of delicious cakes by the new, quick blender procedure.

The electric mixer does the bigger, eggier cakes better, and of course you can't make a good angel-food cake with a blender—it won't whip enough air into the egg whites for that. But the blender can save you much time and energy—and spare you grated knuckles sometimes, too!—on a great number of very nice cakes. Try these recipes and see for yourself.

General Method for Cakes

Have ingredients at room temperature. Use shortening or soft butter for best results. Sift dry ingredients except sugar into a bowl. Put liquids, sugar, shortening and eggs into blender container. Blend about a minute, on the average, scraping down once midway, then pour the liquids over the dry ingredients and mix lightly but thoroughly. A few simple cakes may be made entirely in the blender.

The blender works fast. Watch it!

Icings

The blender turns out butter icings beautifully smooth. Just remember not to overwork your motor with a stiff frosting. When you want a butter icing thicker than the blender will make it without wheezing a little, finish the frosting in a bowl and add the extra confectioners' sugar. Use your rubber spatula, with the blender motor off, to facilitate mixing icings as well as cake batter.

Apple Nut Torte

(9-inch-square pan; 9 portions)

In just seconds you have this good dessert in the oven.

Blender-chop separately, then combine in a bowl

> 1 cup pecans or walnuts
> Sliced apples (cored but not pared) to make 2 cups
> chopped coarse

In blender container put

> 2 eggs
> 1½ cups sugar
> 1 tablespoon vanilla
> ½ teaspoon salt
> ⅔ cup flour
> 3 teaspoons baking powder

Blend until batter is smooth, 45 seconds to 1 minute usually. Turn into bowl with apples and nuts, stir to mix, and bake in buttered pan about 45 minutes at 350°.

Applesauce Cake

(9-by-13-inch pan)

One of the finest.

Sift together into a bowl

> 2 cups cake flour
> ½ teaspoon soda
> 1½ teaspoons baking powder

Place in blender container

> 1½ cups unsweetened applesauce (canned or fresh, page 112)
> 2 tablespoons cocoa
> ¾ teaspoon salt
> 1 teaspoon cinnamon
> ½ teaspoon cloves
> ½ teaspoon nutmeg
> ½ teaspoon allspice
> 2 eggs
> ½ cup shortening
> 1½ cups sugar
> ¾ cup raisins

Switch on the motor and blend until raisins are chopped. Pour over sifted dry ingredients and mix thoroughly. Pour into greased and floured (or wax-paper-lined) pan and bake at 350° for about 45 minutes. I like Coffee Icing for this.

Coffee Icing

(Will frost 9-by-13-inch loaf or two 8- or 9-inch layers)

Place in blender container and blend smooth

> ¼ cup hot water
> 1 teaspoon instant coffee
> 3 tablespoons soft butter
> ⅛ teaspoon salt

Add gradually, with motor running

> About 3 cups confectioners' sugar

Lift some of the frosting with your spatula after adding 3 cups sugar. You may have the right consistency right there. If not, add a little more sugar, or if the frosting seems too thick, add a little hot water. A few drops of vanilla may be added. Or you can flavor with rum extract.

Banana Cake

(Three 8-inch layers)

Moist; a good keeper.

Sift together in a bowl

> 2½ cups cake flour
> 1½ teaspoons baking powder
> 1 teaspoon soda

Place in blender container

> 2 eggs
> ¾ cup shortening
> 4 medium bananas, sliced
> 1½ cups sugar
> 1 teaspoon vanilla
> ¼ teaspoon salt

Blend until smooth and pour over dry ingredients. Mix until just smooth. Pour into greased, floured or wax-paper-lined pans and bake at 375° for about 30 minutes. Whipped cream is the perfect filling and frosting for this cake. Whip it in the blender.

Brazil Nut Torte

(Three 8-inch layers)

This one's a breeze with the blender!

Put Brazil nuts into the container a few at a time and grind fine to make

> 2 cups ground Brazil nuts

Turn ground nuts into a bowl. Place in blender container and beat until light

>6 egg yolks
>½ cup sugar
>¼ teaspoon salt

Beat separately, with rotary beater or egg whisk, until stiff

>6 egg whites

Beat in gradually

>½ cup sugar

Fold nuts into yolk mixture, then whites into the combination. Pour batter into layer pans greased, lined with wax paper and again greased. Bake in moderate oven, 350°, for 35 minutes. Put together when cool with blender-whipped cream.

Butterscotch Cake

(Two 8-inch layers)

Café au lait *in color.*

Sift together into a bowl

>2 cups cake flour
>3 teaspoons baking powder
>1 teaspoon salt

Place in blender container

>½ cup shortening
>¾ cup milk
>1 teaspoon vanilla
>2 eggs
>1½ cups brown sugar

Blend smooth, pour over dry ingredients and mix thoroughly. Bake in greased, floured pans at 350°, moderate oven, for 35 minutes. Cool and put together with Butterscotch Icing.

Butterscotch Icing

(Will frost 8- or 9-inch-square cake, or 2 layers)

Place in warmed blender container

> 2 tablespoons hot milk
> 1 tablespoon light corn sirup
> ¼ cup (½ stick) soft butter
> ½ teaspoon vanilla
> 1 cup brown sugar

Blend until smooth and add gradually

> About 1 cup confectioners' sugar

Blend until smooth and spreadable.

Brown Velvet Spice Cake

(9½-by-5½-inch loaf pan)

Fine texture; fine flavor.

Sift together into mixing bowl

> 2 cups cake flour
> 1½ teaspoons baking powder
> ½ teaspoon salt
> ½ teaspoon soda

Place in blender container

> 1¼ cups sour milk or buttermilk
> 1 egg
> ½ cup shortening
> 1 cup sugar
> 2½ teaspoons cinnamon
> ½ teaspoon nutmeg
> ½ teaspoon allspice
> 2 teaspoons ginger
> 1 tablespoon cocoa

Blend about 1 minute. Pour over sifted ingredients, mix well and turn into greased loaf pan. Bake at 350° for 1 hour. Cool and frost with Raisin Cream Icing.

Raisin Cream Icing

(Will frost loaf cake or 2 layers)

Place in blender container

>About 2 inches outer peeling of orange
>¼ cup orange juice
>¼ cup cream
>1 teaspoon lemon juice
>½ cup raisins

Blend until raisins are fine. Add gradually, while blending

>1½ cups confectioners' sugar

Blend smooth and turn out into bowl with

>1½ cups more confectioners' sugar

Mix smooth. If frosting seems thin, you can add a little more of the sugar, but usually it "sets" a little, within a minute or so, and doesn't need more thickening.

Carrot Pecan Cake

(10-inch tube pan)

Such a flavorsome cake would have been hard work before the advent of the electric blender!

Chop fine in blender and set aside

>1 cup pecans

Place in container

>1¼ cups salad oil
>4 eggs
>2 cups sugar

2 teaspoons cinnamon
1 teaspoon salt

Blend 5 seconds, then add gradually

3 cups sliced raw carrots

Blend just until grated. Pour over, in mixing bowl

2 cups flour
1 teaspoon soda
2 teaspoons baking powder

Mix well and pour into oiled pan. Bake at 325° about 1 hour and 10 minutes. Good with any butter icing or simply sprinkled with confectioners' sugar.

Cinnamon Cake

(Two 8-inch layers)

This is one of the nicest of spice cakes.

Sift together into a bowl

2 cups cake flour
1 teaspoon soda
½ teaspoon salt

Place in the blender container

½ cup shortening
1 cup sour milk or buttermilk, or 1 cup milk plus
    1 tablespoon vinegar
1 tablespoon cinnamon
2 eggs
1¼ cups packed brown sugar

Blend smooth, pour over dry ingredients and mix thoroughly. Spread in 2 greased, floured (or wax-paper-lined) layer pans and bake at 350° about 25 minutes. Almost any of the butter icings is good with Cinnamon Cake. Try Banana Butter Icing.

Banana Butter Icing

(For two 8- or 9-inch layers)

Place in blender container

2 medium-sized bananas, in thirds
1 teaspoon lemon juice
2 tablespoons soft butter
½ teaspoon vanilla
¼ teaspoon salt

Blend smooth and add gradually, working it in with spatula at the last

2½ cups confectioners' sugar

Cinnamon Prune Cake

(9-by-13-inch pan)

Spicy, fruity and moist, this cake keeps well.

In blender container place

3 eggs
¾ cup soft shortening
¼ cup sour cream
¼ teaspoon salt
⅓ cup prune juice
1 cup cooked or canned prunes, well drained
1 cup sugar
3 teaspoons cinnamon
½ teaspoon nutmeg
¼ teaspoon cloves

Blend until ingredients are mixed and prunes are chopped (not until they disappear!). Pour mixture over combination of

2 cups flour
2 teaspoons baking powder
¼ teaspoon soda

Mix well with wooden spoon and turn into oiled pan. Bake at 375° about 35 minutes. Frost in pan with Mocha Icing, page 74. Or serve topped with whipped cream or ice cream.

Cheese Cake Supreme

(Serves 10)

Luscious, delectable, "out of this world"—there aren't enough adjectives to describe this smooth dessert!

Combine and press firmly over bottom and lower sides of 9-inch spring-form pan

> ¾ package zwieback, crushed to crumbs in blender
> ¼ cup soft butter
> ¼ cup sugar

Place in blender container

> 1 cup sweet or sour cream
> 1 teaspoon vanilla
> 4 egg yolks
> ½ cup sugar
> 2 tablespoons flour
> ¼ teaspoon salt

Blend smooth and add in pieces

> 1 pound soft cream cheese

Blend smooth, using rubber spatula as needed. Beat until stiff, then fold in

> 4 egg whites

Pour over crumbs and bake in moderately slow oven, 325°, an hour or until set in the center. Cool and chill before cutting. Wonderful topped with crushed sweetened strawberries, but elegant enough plain. I sometimes simplify things by putting the whole eggs into the blender. The cake isn't quite so fluffy, but tastes equally good.

Glazed Strawberry Cheese Cake

(9-inch spring-form pan)

Less rich than many, it is delicate and divine!

Crust:

Mix well and press over sides and bottom of buttered pan

> 1 cup blender-crumbed zwieback
> ¼ cup sugar
> ½ teaspoon cinnamon
> 3 tablespoons soft butter

Place in blender container

> 4 cups (2 16-ounce cartons) cottage cheese
> 4 eggs
> ½ cup heavy cream
> 1 cup sugar
> ¼ cup flour
> 1 tablespoon lemon juice
> 1 tablespoon vanilla

Blend until smooth and pour into crumb-lined pan. Bake at 350° for 50 minutes. Leave in oven with heat off 30 minutes more. Cool on rack, loosen sides of pan and remove cake. Chill.

Prepare topping:

Mix in a saucepan

> ½ cup sugar
> 4 teaspoons cornstarch
> ½ cup cold water

Cook and stir over low heat until thickened and clear. Cool and add

> 2 or 3 drops red food coloring
> 1 pint halved fresh strawberries

Chill and spoon over top of cheese cake. Chill until serving time.

Chocolate Cake with Pudding Mix

(8-by-8-by-2-inch pan)

Easy to do and very good.

Sift together in a bowl

> 1 cup cake flour
> 1 teaspoon soda
> ½ teaspoon cream of tartar
> ¼ teaspoon salt

Place in blender container

> ½ cup shortening
> 1 cup milk
> 1 teaspoon vanilla
> 2 eggs
> 2 packages chocolate pudding mix (the kind you
> have to cook to make pudding)

Blend until smooth, pour over dry ingredients and mix well.
Bake in well-greased pan lined with wax paper at 350° for 40
to 45 minutes. Cool and frost with Chocolate Icing.

Chocolate Icing

(Enough for 1 square cake or 2 layers)

Place in blender container

> 2 tablespoons soft butter
> 1 teaspoon vanilla
> 2 ounces unsweetened chocolate, melted
> 3 tablespoons hot milk
> ½ teaspoon salt

Blend smooth and add gradually, with motor running

> 2 cups confectioners' sugar
> Add a 3-ounce package of cream cheese to this mix-
> ture for a fluffy, high-piling frosting.

Fresh Coconut Cake

(1 loaf, 9½ by 5½ inches)

A white fruit cake, not too rich, and certainly delicious.

Crack coconut after piercing eyes and draining liquid (save it). Pare off brown parts and blender-grate coconut meat, using 1 cup water in the blender, then draining. Set aside.

In blender container place

> ½ cup coconut water or milk
> ½ cup soft butter
> 1 cup sugar
> 1 teaspoon salt

Blend until smooth and pour over, in a mixing bowl

> 2¼ cups cake flour
> 2 teaspoons baking powder

Mix well and stir in by hand

> 2 cups blender-grated coconut
> ½ pound (1⅓ cups) light raisins (rinsed in hot water
>   and dried on paper towel)
> 1 cup candied cherries, cut in pieces
> ¼ pound candied orange peel, in strips
> ½ pound (1½ cups) slivered blanched almonds

Mix well and fold in

> 4 egg whites, beaten stiff

Turn into greased pan lined with greased heavy brown paper, and bake at 300° for 2½ hours.

Crunch Cake

(2 loaves, 9½ by 5½ inches)

A tender tea cake with an oh-so-good crumb coating. Eat one cake; freeze the second.

Topping:

Blender-crumb vanilla wafers to make

>1½ cups

Chop fine in blender and add to crumbs

>1 cup pecans

Add and blend well with your fingers

>½ cup soft butter
>⅓ cup sugar

Pat on bottoms and sides of the greased pans.

Cake:

Place in blender container

>1 cup milk
>1 cup soft butter
>4 eggs
>2 cups sugar
>2 teaspoons vanilla
>½ teaspoon salt

Whirl smooth in blender, using spatula in surface of mixture as necessary. Pour over mixture of

>2⅔ cups flour
>3 teaspoons baking powder

Mix well, turn into pans over crumb coating and bake at 350° for 1 to 1¼ hours. Turn out on cake racks to cool.

You can make a lemon cake of this by omitting vanilla and adding outer peel of ½ lemon to the contents of the blender.

Devil's Food Cake

(9-inch-square pan, 2 inches deep)

Rich chocolate flavor.

Sift together into a bowl

1¾ cups cake flour
¾ teaspoon salt
1 teaspoon soda

Place in blender container

½ cup shortening
1 cup milk
1 teaspoon vanilla
2 eggs
4 ounces (squares) unsweetened chocolate, melted
1¼ cups sugar

Blend until smooth and pour into dry ingredients. Mix thoroughly. Bake in greased, wax-paper-lined pan at 350° for 50 to 60 minutes. Mocha Icing is wonderful with this cake.

Mocha Icing

(For loaf cake or 2 layers)

Place in blender container

¼ cup hot water
1 teaspoon instant coffee
1 package semisweet chocolate pieces (6 ounces)
⅛ teaspoon salt
½ teaspoon vanilla

Blend until smooth. Add gradually, with motor running

2 cups confectioners' sugar

Date Nut Cake

(8-by-8-by-2-inch pan)

A moist cake that keeps well.

Sift together into a bowl

1½ cups flour
½ teaspoon baking powder
¼ teaspoon salt

Place in blender container and blend smooth

> 1 cup hot water
> 1 tablespoon instant coffee
> 1 cup pitted dates (8-ounce package)
> 1 teaspoon soda

Add

> ½ cup shortening
> ½ cup granulated sugar
> ½ cup brown sugar
> 1 egg
> 1 teaspoon vanilla

Blend smooth, then add and blend 15 seconds

> ½ cup nuts

Pour blended ingredients into dry ingredients, mix thoroughly and turn into greased, wax-paper-lined pan. Bake at 350° about 50 minutes. Good served warm or cold with whipped cream.

Gold Cake

(Two 9-inch layers)

Amazingly light and tender.

Sift together into a bowl

> 1¾ cups cake flour
> 3 teaspoons baking powder
> ¼ teaspoon salt

Place in blender top

> 2 strips outer peel of lemon
> ½ cup shortening
> ½ cup milk
> 1 teaspoon lemon extract

Blend to grate lemon peel. Add

> 8 egg yolks
> 1 cup sugar

Blend thoroughly, about 1 minute. Pour into dry ingredients and mix well. Spread in two greased, floured (or wax-paper-lined) cake pans and bake at 375° for 20 to 25 minutes. Fill with a lemon filling (packaged mix, to make it easy) and frost with Lemon and Orange Icing.

Lemon and Orange Icing

(Enough for two 9-inch layers or three 8-inchers)

Place in blender container

> Outer rind of ½ orange
> 1 strip lemon rind
> 2 tablespoons orange juice
> 2 tablespoons lemon juice
> 3 tablespoons soft butter
> 1 egg yolk
> Dash salt

Blend until smooth and add gradually with motor on

> About 3 cups confectioners' sugar

If motor growls, turn into bowl and add the last cup by hand.

Graham Cracker Cake

(9-by-9-by-2-inch cake)

So speedy to make, and so good to eat!

Crumble a few at a time into the container, and blend until fine

> 12 graham crackers (1 cup, crushed)

Put into a bowl with

> 1 teaspoon salt
> 1 cup cake flour
> 2 teaspoons baking powder

Place in blender container

>1 cup milk
>½ cup shortening
>¾ cup sugar
>2 eggs
>1 teaspoon vanilla

Blend about a minute or until smooth, and add

>1 cup pecans

Blend about 15 seconds to chop nuts. Pour over dry ingredients and stir together lightly. Pour into greased, floured pan and bake at 350° for 30 minutes or until done. Cool on rack and serve with whipped cream or a butter icing.

Jelly Roll

(10½-by-15½-inch shallow pan)

Impossible to make a jelly roll in a blender? Just see for yourself!

Sift together into a bowl

>1 cup cake flour, minus 2 tablespoons
>1¼ teaspoons baking powder
>¼ teaspoon salt

Place in blender container

>4 egg yolks
>3 tablespoons cold water
>1 teaspoon vanilla or lemon extract
>½ cup sugar

Blend until fluffy. In another bowl beat until stiff

>4 egg whites

Gradually beat into the whites

>½ cup sugar

Pour blended mixture into dry ingredients and mix gently but thoroughly. Pour over egg-white meringue and fold together well. Line jelly-roll pan with greased wax paper. Pour in batter. Bake in hot oven, 425°, 12 to 15 minutes. Turn at once onto warm, slightly damp towel. Remove wax paper and trim crusted edges of cake. Spread with

> 1 cup jelly or preserves, any kind

Roll lengthwise, cover with towel and let stand a few minutes. Remove towel and sift confectioners' sugar over top of roll. Serve Jelly Roll in slices, with or without whipped cream.

Lazy Daisy Cake

(9-inch-square loaf)

Has its own scrumptiously good topping!

Sift together into a bowl

> 1 cup cake flour
> 1½ teaspoons baking powder
> ½ teaspoon salt

Place in blender container

> ½ cup hot milk
> 1 cup sugar
> 2 eggs
> 1 teaspoon vanilla
> 1 tablespoon butter

Blend smooth, pour over sifted dry ingredients and mix thoroughly. Bake in greased, floured (or wax-paper-lined) pan at 350° for 30 minutes.

Lazy Daisy Topping

(Covers 9 square inches)

Heat together until melted

> ½ cup butter or margarine
> 1 cup brown sugar

Add, then spread on hot Lazy Daisy Cake

> 6 tablespoons cream
> 1 cup coconut
> 1 cup blender-chopped nuts

Slide cake under the broiler for about 3 minutes until topping is bubbly and lightly browned.

Lemonade Torte

(9-inch spring-form pan)

Moist, lemony and—super!

Blender-grate and turn into bowl together

> ¾ cup almonds (blanched or not)
> Dry bread to make 1½ cups fine crumbs (break slices into pieces to blend)

Add

> 1½ cups sugar
> ¼ teaspoon baking powder
> ¼ teaspoon cinnamon

In blender container put

> Outer peel of 1 lemon
> 1 cup water

Blend until peel is chopped fine. Drain in sieve, saving water. Put peel in bowl with nuts and crumbs.

Beat to a froth (not until stiff)

> 6 egg whites

Mix with contents of bowl and turn into pan. Bake at 350° for 1 hour.

Heat the reserved lemon-water, add

> 2 tablespoons sugar
> Juice of 1 lemon (3 tablespoons)

Pour this mixture over torte while it is still hot.

Maple Sirup Cake

(Two 8-inch layers)

A delicate cake with a "Vermont" flavor.

Sift together into a bowl

> 2 cups cake flour
> ½ teaspoon salt
> 2½ teaspoons baking powder

Place in blender container

> ½ cup shortening
> ¾ cup maple sirup
> 2 eggs
> 1 teaspoon vanilla
> ½ cup sugar

Blend about 1 minute. Add and blend 15 seconds more

> ½ cup butternuts, pecans or walnuts

Pour over dry ingredients and mix well. Bake in greased, floured pans at 375° for 20 to 25 minutes. Cool 5 minutes, turn cakes onto racks to cool and put together and frost with Maple Icing.

Maple Icing

(Enough for 2 layers)

Place in blender container

> ¼ cup soft butter
> ½ cup maple sirup
> ½ teaspoon vanilla

Blend smooth and add gradually without stopping motor

About 2½ cups confectioners' sugar

Moravian Walnut Torte

(3 nine-inch layers)

A delicate party cake such as this requires hand mixing, but the blender is indispensable in preparing the nuts, and can whip cream for the filling.

Blender-grate, ½ cup at a time, and turn into a bowl

1 pound (4½ cups) walnuts

Blender-grate

Yellow outer peel of
1 lemon in
½ cup water

Drain off water and add grated lemon to nuts with

1 teaspoon cinnamon
¼ teaspoon allspice

Beat with mixer or rotary beater, until thick and lemon-colored

12 egg yolks
1 teaspoon vanilla

Gradually beat in

¾ cup sugar

In another bowl whip until glossy points form

12 egg whites

Gradually beat in another

¾ cup sugar

Gradually add nut mixture to beaten yolks, then fold into whites. Turn batter into pans 2 inches deep, greased, lined with waxed paper and again greased. Bake at 350° about 45 minutes. Let stand in pans about 10 minutes, turn out on cake racks, cool and put together with currant jelly and whipped cream.

Orange Gingerbread

(8-inch-square pan)

Just a little different.

Sift into mixing bowl

> 1⅓ cups flour
> 1 teaspoon baking powder
> ½ teaspoon soda
> 1 teaspoon ginger
> ¼ teaspoon cloves
> Dash of salt

Place in blender container

> Outer peel of 1 orange, in pieces
> ½ cup orange juice
> ½ cup molasses
> ¼ cup shortening
> ¼ cup sugar
> 1 egg

Blend mixture about a minute, then pour over dry ingredients and mix lightly. Bake in greased, floured pan 30 minutes at 375° and serve warm with whipped cream or ice cream or with cream cheese softened with a little cream and flavored with a bit of marmalade.

Orange Raisin Cake with Rum

(9-inch-square pan)

Moist, orangey and luscious!

Sift together into a bowl

2 cups cake flour
1 teaspoon baking powder
½ teaspoon salt
½ teaspoon soda

Mix in a separate bowl and let stand

½ cup orange juice
½ cup sugar
2 tablespoons rum

Place in blender container

Outer rind of 2 oranges, cut in strips
½ cup raisins
⅔ cup sour milk or buttermilk
½ cup shortening
1 teaspoon vanilla
2 eggs
1 cup sugar

Blend until smooth. Pour into dry ingredients and mix thoroughly. Bake in greased, wax-paper-lined pan at 350° for 40 to 45 minutes. Remove from oven and pour orange-juice mixture over cake. Serve with whipped cream.

Penuche Cake

(8-by-8-by-2-inch pan)

Everybody's crazy about this cake.

Sift together into a bowl

1⅓ cups cake flour
½ teaspoon salt
½ teaspoon soda
½ teaspoon baking powder
½ teaspoon cinnamon

Place in blender container

½ cup shortening
¾ cup sour milk or buttermilk

       1 egg plus 1 yolk
       1 cup brown sugar

Blend smooth, then pour over dry ingredients and mix thoroughly. Turn into wax-paper-lined greased pan.

Whip until stiff

       1 egg white

Beat in gradually

       ½ cup brown sugar

Spread this meringue on cake batter. Sprinkle with

       ¾ cup blender-chopped pecans

Bake at 350° for 45 minutes.

Plain Two-Egg Cake

(Two 8-inch layers)

A family favorite.

Sift together into a bowl

       2 cups cake flour
       2½ teaspoons baking powder
       ½ teaspoon salt

Place in blender container

       ½ cup shortening
       ½ cup milk
       2 eggs
       1 teaspoon vanilla
       1 cup sugar

Blend about a minute, or until smooth, pour over dry ingredients and mix well. Bake in greased, wax-paper-lined pans at 375° for 25 to 30 minutes. Good with Peanut Butter Icing, chocolate or whatever you like.

Peanut Butter Icing

(Covers two 8-inch layers)

This also makes an elegant ice-cream sauce.

Place in blender container

¼ cup hot milk
¼ cup peanut butter
2 tablespoons soft butter
½ cup brown sugar

Blend smooth and add gradually

About 1½ cups confectioners' sugar

Work frosting with a spatula at the last if it gets too thick to please the blender motor.

Pineapple Upside Down Cake

This popular dessert takes the same batter—it's just the Two-Egg Cake in its Sunday best.

In a 10-inch heavy skillet melt

½ cup butter

Add and stir until dissolved

1 cup brown sugar

Arrange over butter and sugar

6 to 8 drained pineapple slices
6 to 8 maraschino cherries

Pour the plain Two-Egg Cake batter over the mixture and bake 45 to 50 minutes at 350° to 375°. Loosen cake from sides of skillet with a spatula, invert on a large cake plate and serve warm with whipped cream. The same versatile batter turns into cottage pudding if baked in a square 8-inch pan 2 inches deep and dressed with lemon sauce. Or make cupcakes of it—1½ dozen of them—by baking in greased muffin pans at 375° about 20 to 25 minutes.

Snow White Cake

(Two deep 9-inch layers)

This is the perfect birthday cake.

Sift together into a bowl

> 3 cups cake flour
> 3 teaspoons baking powder

Place in blender container

> 1 cup milk
> 1 cup shortening
> 1½ teaspoons vanilla
> 1¼ cups sugar
> ½ teaspoon salt

Blend 2 or 3 minutes. This mixture is very thick. Pour over dry ingredients and mix thoroughly. Beat until foamy

> 6 egg whites

Add gradually and beat until stiff

> ¾ cup sugar

Fold into first mixture. Spread in greased, wax-paper-lined pans and bake 35 minutes in 350° oven. Seven-minute frosting is the usual topper for this. That you can't make in a blender. But the cake is also nice with this Apricot Icing.

Apricot Icing or Glaze

(Enough for 2 layers)

Place in blender container

> 1 cup drained soaked dried apricots
> ¾ cup hot orange juice

Blend smooth, and add gradually

> About 2 cups confectioners' sugar

Walnut Torte

(Two 8-inch layers)

A grand party dessert.

Chop in blender and set aside

> 1 cup walnuts

Sift together into a mixing bowl

> 1 cup flour
> ⅛ teaspoon salt
> 2 teaspoons baking powder

Place in blender container

> ½ cup shortening
> ⅓ cup milk
> ½ teaspoon vanilla
> 4 egg yolks
> ½ cup sugar

Blend about a minute, then pour into dry ingredients and mix well. Pour into greased, wax-paper-lined pans and spread with meringue. To make meringue, beat until stiff with rotary egg beater

> 4 egg whites
> ⅛ teaspoon cream of tartar

Gradually add and beat until glossy

> ¾ cup sugar

Bake in slow oven at 300° for 1 hour. Cool.

Meanwhile, combine, chill for an hour, then whip until stiff

> 1½ cups heavy cream
> ⅓ cup cocoa
> ½ cup sugar

Spread over the torte and serve.

Wonder Sponge Cake

(8- or 9-inch tube pan)

The wonder is such good sponge cake for the investment of only two eggs!

Sift together in a mixing bowl

>1½ cups flour
>½ teaspoon baking powder
>Dash salt

Place in blender container and run motor until these are finely chopped

>1 strip lemon rind (outer peel only)
>1 strip orange rind (all around the orange if you wish)
>⅓ cup orange juice

Add

>⅓ cup water
>2 egg yolks
>1½ cups sugar

Blend smooth, pour over dry ingredients, mix thoroughly and fold in

>2 egg whites, beaten stiff by hand (use a wire whisk)

Pour into ungreased tube pan, bake at 325° about 50 minutes, then invert cake and cool. Serve with crushed sweetened strawberries and whipped cream.

Buttermilk Doughnuts

(3½ dozen)

Fresh from the kettle, they're tender and wonderful!

Place in blender container

>2 eggs
>1 cup buttermilk

1 cup sour cream
1 teaspoon vanilla
1½ cups sugar
½ teaspoon salt

Blend a few seconds until bubbly and pour into a bowl with

6 cups flour
2 teaspoons soda

Mix and stir well. Chill dough. Roll ½ inch thick, cut dough-nuts and fry in deep fat at 365°, turning once, as soon as doughnut is brown. Drain on paper toweling. Roll in confec-tioners' sugar, granulated sugar or mixture of sugar and cinnamon, if you wish.

COOKIES

Almond Cookies

(10 dozen dainty ones, 1½ inches across)

A good refrigerator cooky.

Place in blender container

1 egg
½ cup very soft butter
½ cup sugar
1 teaspoon almond extract
Outer yellow peel from ½ lemon

Blend until creamy. Add gradually

¾ cup unblanched almonds

Blend until almonds are finely ground. Sift together into mixing bowl

2 cups flour
½ teaspoon cinnamon
½ teaspoon cloves
½ teaspoon nutmeg

Add liquids to dry ingredients, stirring until well mixed. Form into long rolls and chill several hours or overnight. Slice and bake on greased cooky sheet 5 to 8 minutes at 350°, moderate oven. Cookies should be only faintly brown. They freeze well, baked or unbaked.

Almond Shortbread

(About 5 dozen cookies)

Use unblanched almonds for these buttery, crunchy goodies.

Grate in blender and set aside

>   1 cup almonds

Cream by hand or in mixer

>   1 cup butter
>   1 teaspoon almond extract
>   ½ cup confectioners' sugar

Mix in by hand

>   2 cups flour

Add almonds. Shape into small balls and flatten slightly with a fork on baking sheets. Bake at 325° about 20 minutes or until tinged with light brown.

Applesauce Cookies

(4 dozen medium size)

Spicy, nutty, fruity—you'll likee!

Chop coarse in blender and place in mixing bowl

>   1 cup nuts

Add

>   1 cup raisins
>   2½ cups flour
>   1 teaspoon soda

½ teaspoon salt
½ teaspoon cinnamon
½ teaspoon cloves
½ teaspoon nutmeg

Place in blender container

1 egg
1 cup thick applesauce
½ cup shortening
1 cup sugar

Blend smooth and turn into flour mixture. Mix with spoon and drop by spoonfuls on greased cooky sheet, allowing 2 inches between cookies. Bake in moderate oven, 350°, about 15 to 20 minutes or until browned.

Banana Oatmeal Cookies

(4 dozen)

Delicious and so easy!

Place in blender container

1 egg
¾ cup shortening
1 cup sugar

Blend until light and fluffy. Add

2 large bananas, cut up (or 3 smaller ones)

Blend until bananas are whipped. Add

½ cup pecans or walnuts

Blend a few seconds until nuts are coarsely chopped. Sift together into mixing bowl

1½ cups flour
1 teaspoon salt
½ teaspoon soda
¼ teaspoon nutmeg
¾ teaspoon cinnamon

Add

      1¾ cups rolled oats

Pour liquid mixture into dry ingredients and stir until smooth. Drop by teaspoonfuls, about 1½ inches apart, onto ungreased cooky sheet. Bake at 400° for 15 minutes or until done.

Bohemian Butter Cookies

(About 5 dozen)

Roll these or use the cooky press.

Place in blender

      2 raw egg yolks
      1 cup very soft butter
      2 hard-cooked egg yolks
      ¾ cup sugar
      Juice of ½ lemon
      Pared outer rind of ¼ lemon

Blend until thoroughly mixed and until rind is finely chopped. Place in mixing bowl

      3½ cups flour
      ¼ teaspoon salt

Stir liquid mixture into dry ingredients. Chill about an hour or until dough is stiff enough to put through cooky press or to roll in small portions. Shape as you like, or roll on floured and sugared board, and cut. Bake at 375° for 10 minutes or until done.

Rich Brownies

(Forty 2-inch squares)

These are the dark, soft ones that everybody loves!

Blender-chop and set aside

      1 cup pecans

Place in blender container

>4 eggs
>¾ cup soft butter
>2 cups sugar
>1 teaspoon vanilla or 1 tablespoon coffee
>   liqueur
>4 ounces melted, partly cooled unsweetened
>   chocolate

Run spatula up and down several times against the sides of the blender, then blend batter smooth, just a few seconds. Pour into a bowl in which you have placed

>1¼ cups flour
>¼ teaspoon salt
>The reserved nuts

Mix until flour disappears, then spread in greased jelly roll pan (10½ by 15½ inches). Bake at 350° for 25 minutes. Mix by hand and spread warm brownies with this icing:

>2 tablespoons melted butter
>2 ounces melted unsweetened
>   chocolate
>1½ cups sifted confectioners' sugar
>3 tablespoons hot water
>2 teaspoons corn sirup
>1 teaspoon vanilla

Use more hot water, if necessary, to make spreadable. Cool frosted brownies and cut in squares.

Carrot Cookies

(4 to 6 dozen)

Orange-speckled, spicy and chewy.

Place in blender container

>½ cup buttermilk
>2 eggs

⅔ cup shortening
1 cup brown sugar
1 teaspoon vanilla

Blend until thoroughly mixed. Sift into mixing bowl

2 cups flour
1 teaspoon baking powder
½ teaspoon soda
½ teaspoon salt
1 teaspoon cinnamon
¼ teaspoon nutmeg
¼ teaspoon cloves

Add to flour mixture

2 cups rolled oats
1 cup grated raw carrots (grated separately in blender)
½ cup blender-chopped nuts

Stir liquid ingredients into dry ones, mixing carefully. Drop dough in small balls from the tip of a spoon onto a greased cooky sheet. Bake at 400° for 12 to 15 minutes.

Cherry Bars

(Pan 9 by 13 inches)

Sponge-textured, pink and pretty.

Place in blender container

2 eggs
1 cup sugar
¼ teaspoon salt
½ teaspoon almond extract

Blend 5 seconds and add

1 cup drained maraschino cherries (8-ounce jar)
½ cup pecans
1 cup flour
1 teaspoon baking powder

With rubber spatula (motor off!) mix lightly by dipping to bottom of container once or twice. Turn on motor and blend just until mixed. By that time cherries and nuts should be chopped. Be sure to use spatula in top of mixture and blend until a vortex forms. Turn batter into greased 9-by-13-inch pan and bake at 350° about 20 minutes, or until done. Cool, cut into bars and roll in confectioners' sugar, or frost the pan with lemon icing (confectioners' sugar thinned with lemon juice).

Swedish Almond Cherry Tarts

(About 3 dozen)

These are dainty filled cooky shells, pretty as a picture.

Cream by hand or in mixer

> 1 cup butter
> ½ cup sugar
> 2 egg yolks

Add and mix until smooth

> 2 cups flour

Set aside. Place in blender container

> 2 tablespoons maraschino cherry
>   sirup
> 1 tablespoon lemon juice
> 2 egg whites
> 1 cup sugar
> 1½ cups blanched almonds

Blend until almonds are ground fine. Press portions of cooky dough into little fluted cooky-tart pans (2¼ inches in diameter) to line them. Put a teaspoonful of the blender mixture into each and top with

> Maraschino cherries, cut in half

Bake the cooky tarts at 350° for 18 to 20 minutes or until browned. Cool and remove from pans (they'll slide out easily if you turn them upside down on a cake rack and tap them lightly).

Chocolate Bonbon Cookies

(2 dozen)

Fudgy sweets, more like candy than cookies.

Chop fine in blender and set aside in a shallow pan

> 1¼ cups nuts

Place in blender container

> 1 egg
> 1 cup evaporated milk
> 2 tablespoons shortening
> ½ cup sugar
> ½ cup flour
> ⅓ cup cocoa
> ¼ teaspoon salt

Blend smooth and turn into top of double boiler. Cook over hot water, stirring constantly until mixture is very stiff, for 15 minutes or longer. Add

> 1 teaspoon vanilla

Drop from a teaspoon into nuts. Roll into balls well coated with nuts and chill until firm.

Chocolate Snowballs

(6 dozen small)

These are rich, buttery cookies, pretty on a holiday tray.

Chop very fine in blender

> 2 cups pecans

Cream together in a bowl

> 1¼ cups butter (soft)
> ⅔ cup sugar

1 teaspoon vanilla
⅛ teaspoon salt
½ cup cocoa

Work in the chopped pecans and

2 cups flour

Chill dough, shape into small balls by rolling between the palms and bake on cooky sheets at 350° for about 20 minutes. Roll in confectioners' sugar.

Chocolate Spice Drops

(6 dozen)

Spice and chocolate—a flavorsome duo!

Place in blender container and blend until thoroughly mixed

2 eggs
⅔ cup sour cream
½ cup soft butter
1½ cups sugar
2 squares (ounces) unsweetened chocolate, melted
and cooled

Sift together into mixing bowl

3 cups flour
1 teaspoon soda
1 teaspoon cloves
1 teaspoon cinnamon
1 teaspoon allspice

Add to flour mixture

1 cup coarse cut nuts (may be chopped in blender
separately)
1 cup raisins

Add liquid mixture to flour and stir until well mixed. Drop from a teaspoon onto an ungreased cooky sheet and bake 18 to 20 minutes at 350°.

Coconut Drop Cookies

(4 dozen)

Tender and flavorsome; made in a jiffy.

Place in blender container

> 2 eggs
> ¼ cup milk
> ⅔ cup soft butter or margarine
> 1 cup brown sugar
> 1 teaspoon vanilla

Blend until light. Place in mixing bowl

> 2 cups flour
> 2 teaspoons baking powder

Add liquid to dry ingredients, stir until mixed and add

> 1 cup coconut (1 can moist kind)

Drop by teaspoonfuls onto greased cooky sheet an inch or more apart. Bake at 350° for 12 to 15 minutes. These are wonderful warm.

Coffee Brandy Cookies

(4 dozen)

These have a crunchy coating and keep well.

Place in blender container

> 2 eggs
> ½ cup shortening
> 1 cup brown sugar
> ¼ cup strong coffee
> 1 teaspoon brandy (or rum) flavoring

Blend well. Place in bowl

> 1½ cups flour
> 1½ teaspoons baking powder
> ¼ teaspoon salt

Stir blended ingredients into flour mixture. Chill several hours. Then roll teaspoonfuls of the soft dough in

> 2 cups wheat flakes, crushed

Place dough on greased cooky sheet, 2 inches apart. Bake at 400° for 12 minutes. The coffee flavor should come through dominantly, so be sure to make double-strength coffee for these, or use 1 teaspoon instant coffee and ¼ cup water.

Coffee Fingers

(About 175 small cookies)

A recipe big enough to enable you to freeze them ahead for the holidays.

Chop very fine in blender, ½ cup at a time, emptying into a bowl

> 4 cups pecans

Add and set aside

> ¾ cup sugar

Cream by hand or in mixer

> 1 pound soft butter
> ¼ cup sugar
> 1 teaspoon almond extract
> 2 teaspoons rum flavoring

Mix well and work in thoroughly

> 5 cups flour

Chill dough and roll small portions at a time, about ¼ inch thick. Cut into strips about ¾ inch wide and 2 inches long. Dip one side of each cooky into

> 3 egg whites, slightly beaten

Dip into the reserved nuts and sugar. Bake the cookies on cooky sheets at 350° for about 8 to 10 minutes or until delicately browned.

Cry Babies

(Makes 6 dozen)

Keep well; good for the children.

Place in container

> 2 eggs
> 1 cup shortening
> 1 cup sugar
> 1 cup molasses
> 1 tablespoon vinegar
> 1 cup hot water
> 1 tablespoon instant coffee

Blend until thoroughly mixed. Sift together into mixing bowl

> 4½ cups flour
> 1 teaspoon ginger
> 2 teaspoons soda
> 1 teaspoon salt

Add liquid ingredients to dry ingredients, stirring until well blended and smooth. Drop from teaspoon onto lightly greased cooky sheet and bake 10 to 12 minutes at 375°. These can be frosted with a dab of confectioners' sugar icing.

Date Balls

(About 32)

Almost a confection, rich and sweet.

Blender-chop fine and set aside

> 1 cup walnuts

Place in blender container

> 2 eggs
> ½ teaspoon salt
> 2 teaspoons lemon extract

½ cup sugar
½ cup light corn sirup
8 ounces (1 cup) pitted dates

Blend until dates are chopped fine. Add and blend just to mix, the nuts and

¾ cup flour

Spread mixture in two buttered 8-inch-square pans, bake at 350° about 20 minutes, then cut into squares. While warm, shape into balls with the palms and roll in

½ cup confectioners' sugar

Fruit Crumb Cookies

(3½ to 4 dozen)

Crisp outside, chewy within. So good!

Simmer until soft

1 cup pitted dates (8 ounces)
1¾ cups dried apricots
1¾ cups water

Place ⅓ of the mixture in the blender at a time and run the motor until you get a soft thick mass. Add 1 tablespoon lemon juice and chill. Meanwhile, combine in mixing bowl

2 cups flour
1 teaspoon soda
¼ teaspoon salt
2 cups quick-cooking oatmeal

Place in blender container

¾ cup soft butter
¾ cup dark-brown sugar
¼ cup light corn sirup
1 teaspoon vanilla

Blend thoroughly. Pour into oatmeal-flour mixture to make a coarse crumbiness. Drop chilled fruit by teaspoons into crumbs and roll about until thickly coated. Place on greased cooky sheet and bake at 350° for 25 minutes.

Ginger Bars

(Makes fifty-six 1½-by-2-inch bars)

Moist; a good keeper.

Place in container

> 2 eggs
> ½ cup shortening
> ½ cup brown sugar
> ½ cup molasses
> ½ cup hot water

Blend thoroughly. Sift into mixing bowl

> 1½ cups flour
> ½ teaspoon cinnamon
> ½ teaspoon nutmeg
> ½ teaspoon ginger
> ½ teaspoon salt
> ½ teaspoon soda

Add liquid mixture to dry ingredients, stirring well until smooth. Pour into a greased jelly-roll pan, 10½ by 15½ inches. Bake at 350° for 18 to 20 minutes. Ice while slightly warm with a thin confectioners' sugar icing flavored with lemon. Cut into bars when cool.

Gold Bricks

(20 squares)

Moist and delicious!

Place in blender container

> 2 eggs
> ½ cup buttermilk
> ½ cup soft butter

1 cup granulated sugar
½ cup brown sugar
Outer peel of ¼ orange

Blend until light and fluffy. Then add

1 cup pecans
1 cup cooked apricots

Blend until nuts are coarsely chopped. Sift together into mixing bowl

1½ cups flour
1 teaspoon baking powder
1 teaspoon baking soda
¼ teaspoon salt

Pour liquid mixture into dry ingredients and stir until blended. Spread in a greased pan, 9 by 13 inches. Bake at 350° for 25 minutes or until done. Cool. Cut into 20 squares. Sprinkle top with confectioners' sugar, or serve with whipped cream.

Grandma's Filbert Cookies

(5 dozen small ones)

Very, very good, and done entirely by blender.

Grind in blender a cup at a time, until very fine, then set aside

3 cups filberts

Place in container

2 eggs
1 cup sugar
Dash of salt
½ teaspoon vanilla

Blend until thick and lemon colored. Add to ground nuts and mix well. Chill for at least 3 hours. Roll small portions of dough into small balls the size of hickory nuts. Place on greased cooky sheets and bake at 325° for 15 minutes or until done. While still warm, roll in confectioners' sugar.

Hedgehogs

(5 dozen)

Chewy goodies that travel well to college.

Blender-chop and set aside

>2 cups walnuts or pecans

Place in blender top

>2 eggs
>1 cup brown sugar
>8 ounces pitted dates (1 cup)

Blend until dates are chopped rather fine. Add the nuts and

>1 cup shredded or flake coconut

Shape mixture into rolls about 1 inch long and ½ inch thick. Roll each cooky in bowl containing

>1 cup more coconut

Bake cookies on greased cooky sheets at 350° for 15 minutes.

Honey Date Bars

(2 dozen)

So simple to do, and so good!

Place in blender container

>2 eggs
>3 tablespoons shortening
>¾ cup honey

Blend until creamy. Then add gradually

>1 cup pitted dates (8 ounces)

When thoroughly chopped add quickly and blend just a second or two

> ⅔ cup nuts

Mix in a bowl

> ¾ cup flour
> ¾ teaspoon baking powder
> ¼ teaspoon salt

Add honey mixture to dry ingredients and stir until thoroughly combined. Pour into well-greased 8-inch-square pan. Bake at 350° for 30 minutes or until golden brown. Cut into bars 1 by 2½ inches. Dip ends in confectioners' sugar. These are moist and chewy. You'll like them.

Lemon Drops

(5 dozen tea cookies)

You'll make these again and again!

Mix in a bowl

> 2 cups flour
> 1 tablespoon baking powder

Place in blender container

> 1 small lemon, seeded, quartered
> ¼ cup water

Blend until lemon is fine. Add

> ½ cup shortening
> 1 egg
> 1 cup sugar
> ¾ teaspoon salt

Blend until smooth. Pour over flour and baking powder, and mix well. Drop by level tablespoonfuls onto greased cooky sheet and bake at 400° for 8 minutes. These are tartly flavored lemon cookies, the kind everybody'll want the recipe for.

Frosted Molasses Creams

(2 jelly-roll pans full)

This is one of my favorites.

Sift into a bowl

> 4 cups flour
> ¼ teaspoon salt
> 2 teaspoons cinnamon
> ½ teaspoon ginger
> 2 teaspoons soda

Place in blender container

> 1 cup warm water
> 1 cup molasses
> 2 eggs
> 1 cup shortening
> 1 cup sugar

Blend smooth and pour over dry ingredients. Stir and mix well. Turn into two large, flat pans (10½ by 15½ inches) and bake 15 to 20 minutes at 350°. Cool, frost with a butter icing (Lemon and Orange Icing, page 76, is good) and cut into bars. This is a large recipe and can be neatly cut in half if you like. At our house frosted creams are so popular that even two pans don't last any time at all.

Oatmeal Apple Surprises

(4 dozen 2 inches across)

No grinding of those apples this way!

Mix in a bowl

> 1½ cups flour
> 1 teaspoon baking powder
> ½ teaspoon soda
> 1½ cups rolled oats

Place in blender container

> ¼ cup milk

Slice in, with motor running

> 2 apples, cored but not pared

Add

> ¾ cup raisins

Blend until chopped. Add

> ½ cup shortening
> 1 egg
> 1 cup sugar
> ½ teaspoon salt
> ¼ teaspoon cloves
> ½ teaspoon nutmeg
> 1 teaspoon cinnamon
> 2 tablespoons cocoa

Blend until mixed. Add

> ¾ cup nuts

Blend just a few seconds. Pour over dry ingredients, stir to mix and chill 1 hour. Drop by teaspoonfuls onto greased cooky sheet. Bake in moderate oven, 375°, for 12 to 15 minutes. No work at all, was it?

Orange Coconut Cookies

(2 dozen)

They're nice for a tea party.

Mix in a bowl

> 1⅔ cups cake flour
> ¼ teaspoon soda

Place in blender container

> 1 strip orange rind (outer peel)
> 1 strip lemon rind

1 tablespoon lemon juice
3 tablespoons orange juice
1 egg
½ cup shortening
⅔ cup sugar
¼ teaspoon salt

Blend until mixture is smooth. Without stopping motor add gradually and blend a few seconds

1 cup coconut, shredded or flake

Turn blended mixture into flour and stir to mix well. Drop cookies 2 inches apart on greased baking sheet and bake 12 to 15 minutes at 350°. It's gilding a lily to frost these good cookies, but if you like golden lilies, mix a tablespoon of butter, a tablespoon of orange juice, a squeeze of lemon and a little grated rind with 1⅓ cups sifted confectioners' sugar, and top when right out of the oven.

Orange Drops

(5 dozen)

Sugar-coated and delightful!

Blender-chop and set aside

¾ cup pecans

Place in blender container and blend until smooth

½ cup buttermilk
2 eggs
¾ cup shortening
1½ cups brown sugar
1 teaspoon vanilla
Yellow rind of ½ orange

Sift into mixing bowl

3 cups flour
2 teaspoons baking powder

½ teaspoon soda
¼ teaspoon salt

Add nuts and blended ingredients to flour mixture and stir until combined. Drop by teaspoonfuls onto greased cooky sheet. Bake at 350° for 15 minutes or until delicately browned. Remove from pan. While still hot, dip tops into icing made by combining ½ cup sugar, 3 tablespoons orange juice and 1½ teaspoons grated orange rind.

Pecan Applesauce Drops

(About 5 dozen)

These goodies will keep well—if you can keep them!

In blender container place

1 cup applesauce, canned or fresh (p. 112)
2 eggs
½ cup soft shortening
1 cup sugar
1 teaspoon vanilla
1 teaspoon cinnamon
½ teaspoon nutmeg
¼ teaspoon salt
½ cup pecans

Blend until pecans are chopped. Mix with combination of

2 cups flour
½ teaspoon soda

Stir to combine well. Drop cookies from teaspoon onto greased cooky sheets, leaving about 2 inches between cookies. Bake 8 to 10 minutes at 375°.

Sour Cream Cookies

(5 dozen fat ones or 10 dozen tea size)

Umm! Just like Grandma made!

Place in blender container

> 1 egg
> 1 cup sour cream
> 1 teaspoon vanilla or ½ teaspoon lemon extract, or
>   pared outer rind of ½ lemon
> 1 cup soft butter
> 2 cups brown or white sugar, or 1 cup each

Blend ingredients to a soft creamy texture. Sift together into mixing bowl

> 4½ cups flour
> 1 teaspoon baking powder
> ½ teaspoon soda
> ¼ teaspoon salt

Pour liquid mixture into dry ingredients and stir smooth. Chill dough, then roll on lightly floured and sugared board. Sprinkle with sugar, roll in very lightly and cut cookies. Bake in a 375° oven about 10 to 12 minutes or until lightly browned.

Sugar Cookies

(9 dozen little ones)

Crisp and fine-flavored.

Place in blender container

> Juice of 1 lemon (3 tablespoons)
> ½ cup milk
> 1 pound very soft butter
> 1½ cups sugar
> Outer peel of ½ lemon

Blend until well mixed. Sift together into mixing bowl

> 5 cups flour
> 5 teaspoons baking powder
> ¼ teaspoon salt

Add liquids to flour mixture and stir until well blended. Round up dough, wrap in wax paper and chill. Roll out small portions of dough at a time, keeping the rest cold. Roll very thin, using as little flour as possible on pastry cloth and rolling pin. Cut with small cooky cutters. Place on ungreased cooky sheets and sprinkle with sugar—maybe colored sugar?—and bake in a hot oven, 400°, until lightly browned, about 8 minutes. These are very, very good and very, very simply made by blender.

Wine Fruit Bars

(10½-by-15½-inch pan; will make eighty-eight 1-by-2-inch bars)

An excellent holiday cooky.

Place in blender container

    1 cup evaporated milk
    ¼ cup port or any other sweet wine
    ¾ cup shortening
    1 cup sugar
    ½ teaspoon salt
    ½ teaspoon cinnamon
    ¼ teaspoon nutmeg
    ¼ teaspoon cloves
    ¼ teaspoon ginger
    1 strip outer peel of lemon

Blend well, then add

    ¼ cup candied pineapple, diced
    ¼ cup candied cherries
    ¼ cup candied orange peel
    ½ cup citron, diced
    ½ cup nuts

Blend until these ingredients are chopped. Stir into mixture of

    3 cups flour
    1 teaspoon soda

Spread evenly in shallow greased pan, or about 1 inch thick on greased baking sheet. Bake in 350° oven about 30 minutes. Let cool in pan. Frost with a lemon-flavored confectioners' sugar icing and cut into bars when frosting has set.

5

Desserts

The electric blender cuts preparation time in half for many desserts and makes it easy for us to do such things as grind nuts, grate coconut and purée apricots, tedious procedures before the advent of a blender—so tedious, in fact, that it often was easier to select another recipe than to make the dessert we would really have liked.

Everybody loves desserts, including me, and I find it hard not to go a little haywire in my selections for this book. After all, there must be some limitation! So you won't find here all of the luscious things that my staff at the *Chicago Tribune* and I have been able to make in the blender. But these recipes will show you how to adapt your own favorites to this new, speedy, labor-saving method.

SOME FINE PUDDINGS AND MISCELLANEOUS DESSERTS

Applesauce

(About 2 cups)

The flavor is so fresh!

Wash, cut in halves and core

3 or 4 large apples (juicy, fine-flavored ones)

Slice into bowl containing

> ½ teaspoon salt
> 2 cups water

(This is to prevent discoloration of apples.) Place in blender

> ¼ cup fruit juice or water
> ½ cup sugar (amount depends upon sweetness of apples used)

Start motor and drop in apple slices a few at a time, blending until they are chopped very fine. Stop motor and use spatula once or twice to scrape down sides of container. This sauce is meant to be eaten raw, and should be eaten soon because it darkens on standing. If you prefer a cooked sauce, you can skip the salt-water bath, make the sauce and bring it to a boil. The amount of sugar to use will vary with your choice of apples. Drop 2 tablespoons of red cinnamon candies into the blender with the sauce if you like cinnamon applesauce of a nice pink color.

Apricot Bavarian Cream

(10 to 12 servings)

Looks and tastes luscious!

Place in container

> 1½ tablespoons unflavored gelatin
> ½ cup hot water

Blend to dissolve gelatin. Add

> 2 egg yolks
> ¾ cup sugar
> ¼ teaspoon salt
> 1 cup cooked apricots, drained
> 2 cups juice (liquid from the cooked apricots plus water to make 2 cups)
> 1 teaspoon lemon juice

Blend until apricots are completely broken up and liquefied. Pour into bowl. Chill until mixture begins to thicken. Fold in

> 2 egg whites, beaten stiff
> 1½ cups whipping cream, whipped in blender

Pour into a mold and chill until firm.

Avocado Cream

(6 to 8 servings)

Pale green, creamy and luscious.

Place in blender container

> Juice of 2 limes
> Diced meat of 3 large ripe avocados
> ¾ cup confectioners' sugar

Blend until smooth. Fold carefully into

> 1 quart slightly softened vanilla ice cream

Serve at once. The dessert may be frozen but is much more appealing creamy. It should have the consistency of whipped cream.

Minted Cantaloupe Dessert

(8 servings or more)

A blender will get all the flavor from fresh mint!

Place in blender container

> ½ cup sugar
> ⅛ teaspoon salt
> 1½ teaspoons cornstarch
> 1 cup hot water
> 6 or 8 leafy stems of mint

Blend until mint is very fine. Cook and stir over low heat until sauce thickens and clears, stirring constantly. Cool. Pour over

1½ quarts cantaloupe balls

Chill and serve in cocktail glasses. A mixture of melons may be used—cantaloupe, honeydew and watermelon. Sauce is good on almost any mixture of fresh or fresh and canned fruits.

Chocolate Cooky Pudding

(12 servings)

Fluffy, delicate, easily made for a party, but rich, so keep the portions small!

Crush in blender and empty into a bowl

> ½ pound chocolate sandwich-type cookies (to make 2 cups of crumbs)

Rinse blender container and place in it

> ¼ cup sugar
> 2 tablespoons plain gelatin
> ⅛ teaspoon salt
> ⅔ cup hot water

Blend to dissolve gelatin. Cool. In a medium size mixing bowl place

> 5 egg whites

Beat until soft peaks form, using whisk or rotary beater. Beat in gradually

> ½ cup sugar

Fold cooled gelatin mixture into egg whites along with

> 2 teaspoons vanilla
> 2 cups heavy cream, whipped in blender

Place about two-thirds of the cooky crumbs in a baking dish about 8 by 12 inches in size, scattering them evenly. Turn pudding mixture into the dish, spreading it evenly. Top with remaining crumbs. Chill several hours or overnight.

Chocolate Soufflé

(6 servings)

Luncheon fare for guests.

Prepare in blender and set aside

½ cup fine dry crumbs (use toasted bread)

Place in container

¾ cup milk
2 tablespoons flour
2 tablespoons soft butter
5 egg yolks
1½ squares chocolate, cut in pieces
½ cup sugar

Blend until smooth and pour into saucepan. Cook and stir until thickened and smooth over moderate heat or in top of double boiler. Cool and add

Reserved crumbs
1 teaspoon vanilla or 2 tablespoons rum

Fold into

5 egg whites beaten stiff with
¼ teaspoon salt
½ teaspoon cream of tartar

Bake in greased casserole set in pan of hot water for 1¼ to 1½ hours at 300°. Serve at once with plain or whipped cream or custard sauce.

Baked Orange Custard

(Six servings)

Any custard is easily mixed in the blender.

Place in blender container

4 eggs
¼ teaspoon salt
⅓ cup sugar
Pared outer rind of ½ large orange
¼ teaspoon lemon extract

Blend a few seconds, then add gradually at low speed

2 cups hot milk

Pour into 1½-quart casserole with

2 more cups hot milk

Stir gently and place dish in a pan of hot water. Bake at 350°
about 35 minutes or until firm in the center. Chill and serve
plain or with crushed sweetened peaches or berries.

Cocoa Bread Pudding

(6 servings)

A light, delicate custard version.

Prepare in blender and set aside

1 cup fine fresh bread crumbs

Place in blender container

¾ cup sugar
⅓ cup cocoa
½ teaspoon salt
8 ounces (1 cup) pitted dates
2 cups scalded milk

Blend to cut dates fine. Add and blend a few seconds

2 eggs
½ cup walnuts

Turn into bowl with crumbs, mix well, then pour into buttered
baking dish about 7 by 11 inches. Bake at 350° for 50 minutes
or until a knife inserted in the center of the pudding comes
out clean. Serve warm with chocolate sauce.

Orange Bread Pudding

(6 servings)

Light textured, custardy and very orangey.

Crumb in blender (not too fine) bread to make

> 2 cups coarse crumbs

Empty into bowl and add

> 2 cups milk
> 1 cup currants

In blender container place

> 1 cup orange juice
> Outer peel (no white part) 1 orange
> ¼ teaspoon salt
> ½ cup sugar

Blend until orange peel is very fine. Add and blend just a few seconds

> 3 eggs

Pour over crumbs and milk, adding

> 2 tablespoons melted butter

Bake in buttered casserole or pan about 9 by 12 inches, set in a shallow pan of water, at 350° about 40 minutes or until silver knife inserted in center comes out clean. Serve warm with Orange Sauce, page 293.

Danish Apple Cake

(8 servings)

Not too rich.

Crumb in blender a few pieces at a time and empty into bowl

> 6 ounces zwieback (1 package)

Mix with ¼ cup melted butter. Place in blender

> ¼ cup water
> ½ cup sugar
> 1 teaspoon cinnamon
> 1 tablespoon lemon juice

Switch on motor, then add gradually and chop fairly fine

> 1½ pounds (about 5½) unpared, cored apples, in pieces

Line a buttered bread pan with wax paper. Bring paper up to top of pan to facilitate removal. Place a layer of crumbs on bottom and add a layer of apple mixture. Repeat until all ingredients are used, ending with crumb layer. Bake in a moderate oven, 350°, for 15 minutes. Cool. Chill for several hours or overnight. Unmold and coat with whipped cream, or cut in squares and top with whipped cream. This dessert is not overly sweet and for that reason is an excellent follow-up to a rather hearty entree.

Date Crunch

(9 servings)

Not a dissenting vote on this one!

In blender container place

> 1 cup or 1 package (8 ounces) pitted dates
> ½ cup sugar
> 1 cup boiling water

Blend until mixture is like soft jam. Add and blend until chopped

> ½ to 1 cup pecans

Cream together

> ½ cup butter
> 1 cup firmly packed dark brown sugar

Add and mix until crumbly

> 1 cup flour
> 1 teaspoon baking powder
> 1 cup rolled oats (blender chopped, if you wish)

Pat half the crumb mixture into buttered 8-inch-square pan; cover with the date mixture. Top with rest of crumbs. Bake at 325° for 45 minutes. Serve warm topped with mixture of

> 1 cup heavy cream, blender-whipped
> ¼ teaspoon cinnamon
> ½ teaspoon vanilla

Date Torte

(9-inch-square pan, 9 squares)

Ever hear of anyone not liking it?

Place in blender container

> 1 cup warm water
> 1 tablespoon butter
> 2 eggs
> 1 cup sugar
> 1 cup or 1 package (8 ounces) dates

Blend until smooth and add

> 1 cup nuts

Blend just a second or two to chop nuts. Sift into bowl

> 1 teaspoon soda
> 1 cup flour

Fold in blended mixture. Turn into wax-paper-lined, greased pan. Bake in slow oven, 300°, for 45 to 55 minutes. Cut into squares when cool and serve with cream whipped in the blender.

Coconut Macaroon Dessert

(16 servings)

Ever so easy; ever so luscious!

Place in top of double boiler over hot water

> 1 pound marshmallows
> ½ cup milk

When marshmallows are melted, cool them. Crush in blender and empty into a bowl (crush a handful at a time)

> ¾ to 1 pound coconut macaroons (to make 3 to 4 cups of crumbs)

Rinse blender container and whip in it

> 2 cups heavy cream

Fold cream into marshmallow mixture along with

> 1 can (1 pound 4½ ounces) crushed pineapple, well drained

Sprinkle two-thirds of cooky crumbs over bottom of 9-inch spring-form pan, add pineapple-marshmallow mixture, and top with remaining crumbs. Refrigerate overnight before un-molding and cutting.

Hawaiian Coconut Pudding

(9 squares or 6 servings of pudding)

It's called Haupia in Honolulu.

Grate fresh coconut in the blender to make

> 6 cups grated coconut (see page 358)

Add

> 3 cups hot milk and coconut water

Place in cheesecloth until all liquid is extracted. Squeeze

firmly. Coconut, which should be dry, is discarded. Place 1 cup liquid in blender and add

> 6 tablespoons cornstarch
> 6 tablespoons sugar

Blend smooth and add to rest of liquid in saucepan and cook until thick. Pour into 8-inch-square pan and chill until firm. Cut into squares and serve. In Hawaii these squares are served on ti leaves and eaten with the fingers. If you'd rather have a creamy pudding, use only half the cornstarch and serve in sherbet glasses. Pudding can be flavored with vanilla or rum if you like.

Coffee Rum Cream

(12 servings)

A party dessert topped with crushed peanut brittle.

In blender container place

> 1 cup sugar
> 2½ tablespoons plain gelatin
> 2 tablespoons instant coffee
> 1 cup boiling water

Blend until gelatin and sugar are dissolved. Add

> 1 cup milk
> ¼ cup rum
> ⅛ teaspoon salt

Blend a few seconds, and turn into a pan or bowl. Chill until mixture begins to thicken. Meanwhile whip in blender

> 2 cups heavy cream

Whip with wire whisk

> 2 egg whites

Fold cream and egg whites into partly jelled mixture and turn into a large mold or individual molds. Chill overnight. Blender-crush peanut brittle to make

1 cup peanut brittle crumbs

Whip in blender

1 cup heavy cream

Unmold dessert or individual desserts and serve topped with whipped cream and sprinkled with peanut brittle.

Nougat Pudding

(8 servings)

Save out a little of the whipped cream to garnish the delicious pudding, if you wish.

Blender grate

1 cup almonds (blanched or unblanched)

Stir in heavy skillet over low heat until melted and caramelized

1 cup sugar

Stir in almonds, then

1 cup milk

Simmer and stir until sugar melts again, 2 or 3 minutes. Add small amount of hot mixture to

2 eggs, beaten slightly

Stir vigorously and return mixture to skillet. Cook and stir gently 2 minutes. Add and stir to dissolve

1 tablespoon plain gelatin which has been softened in
¼ cup cold water

Cool mixture until it begins to stiffen. Fold in

2 cups heavy cream, blender-whipped
1 teaspoon vanilla

Turn into a large mold or individual molds. Chill until firm.

Lemon Cracker Pudding

(6 servings)

Simple but good!

Place in blender container

> 2 tablespoons water
> ½ small lemon, in pieces

Blend fine. Add

> 12 soda crackers, square kind
> 1 cup scalded milk

Blend until smooth and add

> 1 cup more scalded milk
> 2 tablespoons butter
> ½ teaspoon salt
> ¾ cup sugar

Without stopping motor add

> 2 egg yolks

Turn into greased baking dish and bake at 350° for 45 minutes. Remove from oven and top with meringue. To make meringue, beat with egg beater until stiff

> 2 egg whites

Then beat in

> ¼ cup sugar
> 1 tablespoon lemon juice

Return to oven for 15 minutes.

Nesselrode Pudding

(6 servings)

This lovely concoction inspires "Oohs" and "A-ahs," also "Yumms."

Chop cherries in blender to make

> ½ cup chopped candied cherries

Set aside and crush in blender

> 1 dozen almond macaroons

Add to cherries and chop in blender

> ½ cup nuts

Add to cherries and macaroon crumbs. Place in container

> ½ cup hot milk
> 1 tablespoon plain gelatin

Blend to dissolve gelatin. Add

> 1 cup scalded milk
> 3 egg yolks
> ⅛ teaspoon salt
> ¼ cup sugar

Blend a few seconds. Turn into top of double boiler and cook until custardy. Add nuts, macaroons, cherries and

> 1 teaspoon vanilla
> Few drops almond extract

Cool. Fold in

> 2 egg whites, beaten stiff

Pour into mold rinsed with cold water. Chill until firm.

Nut Pudding

(6 servings)

Velvety, cakelike texture, and so good!

Place in container

> ½ cup hot cream
> 1 package (6 ounces) semisweet chocolate pieces
> 2 teaspoons vanilla

Blend smooth. Add

    ¼ cup diced candied orange peel

Blend until chopped fine. Add

    4 egg yolks
    ¼ cup sugar

Blend a few seconds and add

    1 cup walnuts

Blend just enough to chop. Fold into

    4 egg whites, beaten stiff

Pour into buttered 1½-quart soufflé dish. Bake in moderate oven, 350°, for 30 minutes. Serve plain or topped with whipped cream.

Peppermint Candy Pudding

(8 servings)

Easy and good.

Crush in blender and set aside

    ½ pound vanilla wafers (to make 2 cups crumbs)

Quarter with scissors and set aside

    ½ pound marshmallows

Chop in blender and add to marshmallows

    ⅔ cup pecans

Crush fine in blender peppermint candy to make

    1 cup crushed peppermint candy

Whip in blender

    1 cup heavy cream

Fold candy, cream into marshmallow-nut mixture.

Line 7-by-10-inch pan with wafer crumbs, cover with marshmallow mixture and top with more crumbs. Chill overnight or for several hours.

Persimmon Dessert

(6 servings)

An unusual treat which may be made a day early.

Purée in blender

> 2 ripe Japanese persimmons, adding
> 1 cup sugar
> ⅛ teaspoon salt

Turn into a bowl and add

> 1½ cups miniature marshmallows
> 1½ cups graham cracker crumbs (packaged or blender made)
> ½ cup blender-chopped walnuts
> ½ cup cream, blender-whipped

Mix lightly and turn into six individual molds. Chill until firm. Unmold and serve plain or garnished with more whipped cream.

Pineapple Mint Cheese Cake

(8 servings)

Flavored with liqueurs for special guests.

Crumb in blender chocolate wafers to make

> 1¼ cups chocolate wafer crumbs

Add

> ⅓ cup melted butter

Press into bottom and on sides of 8-inch spring-form pan. In blender container place

      2 eggs
      3 tablespoons white crème de menthe
      1 tablespoon white crème de cacao
      ½ cup sugar
      11 ounces cream cheese, at room temperature (1
          8-ounce package, plus 1 3-ounce package)

Blend to smooth, fluffy mixture and turn into prepared pan. Bake at 350° for 25 minutes. Cool.

Mix by hand

      1 tablespoon cornstarch
      1 tablespoon pineapple sirup

Add to remainder of

      1 can (1 pound 4 ounces) crushed pineapple

Cook until thickened. Cool and spread on cheese cake. Chill.

FROZEN DESSERTS

Blender-made ice creams are exciting. No longer do you have to melt marshmallows for that velvet texture—you just blend them. The fruit is chopped or puréed, as you wish it; the nuts are chopped; the cinnamon candies dissolved without benefit of cooking. It's all so quick and easy, your dessert is made in nothing flat. Best of all, flavors are perfectly combined and smooth textures achieved when the blender prepares a dessert for the freezer.

Apple Ice Cream

(6 servings)

Fresh-apple flavor; a pretty pink.

Whip in blender

      1 cup heavy cream

Turn into a bowl.

Place in container of blender

⅓ cup lemon juice

Start blender and then slice in

3 apples, cored

Blend until smooth. Add

16 marshmallows, soft (¼ pound)
⅓ cup sugar
½ teaspoon peppermint extract
A few drops red coloring (optional)

Blend thoroughly. Fold apple mixture into whipped cream. Tint mixture with a few drops of red food coloring. Place in refrigerator tray and freeze at coldest temperature.

Cinnamon Apple Ice Cream

(6 servings)

Made with apple jelly.

Whip in blender

1 cup heavy cream

Turn into a bowl.

Place in container of blender

¼ cup red cinnamon candies (2-ounce bottle)
¼ cup milk, scalded

Let stand 5 minutes. Then blend until candies dissolve. Add

½ cup milk
½ cup apple jelly
3 egg whites

Blend a few seconds. Fold mixture into whipped cream. Pour

into refrigerator tray, freeze to a mush, remove to chilled bowl and beat with rotary beater. Return to tray; freeze firm.

Frozen Apricot Cream

(5 servings)

What an easy way to fame as a hostess!

Blender-whip and transfer to a bowl

> 1 cup heavy cream

In blender container place

> Drained apricots from 1 can (1 pound 14 ounces)
> ½ cup sirup from apricots
> ½ cup confectioners' sugar
> 2 tablespoons orange liqueur

Blend until smooth. Fold into whipped cream, transfer to refrigerator tray and freeze until firm. Serve in sherbet glasses garnished with a few

> Sweetened raspberries or strawberries

Avocado Lemon Sherbet

(4 to 6 servings)

Unusual, delightful!

Place in blender container

> 3 strips orange rind
> ⅓ cup lemon juice

Blend to grate rind. Add

> 1½ avocados, peeled
> 1 cup milk
> ⅛ teaspoon salt
> ⅔ cup confectioners' sugar

Blend smooth. Pour into refrigerator tray and freeze, stirring once or twice during freezing. This is a pleasant accompaniment for chicken or seafood, and is a perfect sherbet to serve on a fruit plate with melon, berries and other fresh fruits. It's also nice for dessert.

Bisque Tortoni

(12 servings)

Smooth, creamy, delicious!

Mix and boil to 236° by candy thermometer

> ¾ cup sugar
> ¼ cup water

Mix in top of double boiler

> 5 egg yolks, slightly beaten
> 3 tablespoons water
> ⅛ teaspoon salt

Pour hot sirup over egg yolks, beating constantly. Cook over boiling water, stirring frequently, until mixture is thick. Cool. Stir in

> 3 tablespoons sherry
> 1 tablespoon vanilla

Chill. Whip in blender

> 2 cups heavy cream

Fold into chilled mixture and turn into chilled paper cups. Sprinkle with

> ½ cup toasted salted almonds, chopped fine in blender

Freeze until firm.

Frozen Cheese with Strawberry Sauce

(4 servings)

Easy as pie, and as good.

Place in blender container

> 1 cup cottage cheese
> 1 tablespoon lemon juice
> 1 strip outer peel of lemon
> ½ cup sugar
> 1 cup dairy sour cream

Blend smooth, turn into refrigerator tray and freeze at coldest point until firm around the edges. Stir with spoon until smooth. Freeze firm. Serve in squares with saucing of

> 1 package frozen strawberries, thawed, or 1 pint sweetened fresh berries

Cranberry Marshmallow Velvet

(6 servings)

Creamy texture, delightful flavor!

Place in container

> 1 9-ounce can crushed pineapple and juice
> 2 tablespoons lemon juice
> Few grains salt
> 1 cup heavy cream
> ¼ pound (about 16) marshmallows (soft)

Blend thoroughly. Then add

> 1 pound can whole cranberry sauce (1¾ cups)

Blend thoroughly. Freeze about 3 hours in refrigerator tray.

Frozen Rum and Fruit Pudding

(6 to 8 servings)

A party dessert.

Whip in blender

> 1 cup heavy cream

Turn into a bowl.

Place in container of blender

> 1 cup scalded milk
> 16 marshmallows (¼ pound)

Blend until smooth. Without stopping blender, add in order

> 1 9-ounce can crushed pineapple, drained
> ¾ cup maraschino cherries, drained (1 8-ounce bottle)
> ½ cup pitted dates
> 1 tablespoon rum
> ½ cup pecan halves

Blend about 15 seconds after nuts are added. Fold into cream. Pour into refrigerator tray and freeze at coldest temperature, stirring once during process. Brandy or your favorite liqueur may be used in place of the rum. This dessert can be frozen in a tray lined with cooky or graham-cracker crumbs.

Graham Cracker Ice Cream

(4 to 6 servings)

Made quick as a wink.

Place in blender container

> 2 cups coffee cream
> 8 graham crackers, broken up

½ cup sugar
½ teaspoon black walnut or maple flavoring

Blend smooth. Break into container a few at a time

8 more graham crackers

Blend until mixed. Pour into refrigerator tray and freeze at coldest temperature to a mush. Remove from tray to chilled bowl, beat with egg beater, return to tray and finish freezing.

Instant Cranberry Pineapple Sherbet

(4 servings)

One, two, three, EAT!

Place in blender container

¼ cup cold water
½ cup canned whole cranberry sauce
Frozen pineapple chunks from 14-ounce can, cut into 6 or 8 pieces

Blend until sherbety. Overblending liquefies mixture. Watch it.

Frozen Lemon Cream

(8 servings)

Really lemony and coated with crumbs and nuts.

Blender-crush and empty into bowl vanilla wafers to make

1 cup vanilla wafer crumbs

Blender-chop and empty into same bowl

¼ cup pecans

Rinse blender top and place in it

1 egg
2 egg yolks

Outer rind of 1 lemon
3 tablespoons lemon juice
½ cup sugar

Blend a few seconds, then empty into saucepan and cook over hot water or gently heat, stirring constantly, until mixture thickens. Add, then cool

1 tablespoon butter

Whip until stiff, using wire whisk

2 egg whites

Blender-whip

1 cup heavy cream

Fold egg whites and cream into lemon mixture. Sprinkle half the cooky crumbs and nuts over bottom of refrigerator tray, add lemon mixture and top with remaining crumbs. Freeze until firm. Slice to serve.

Mango Ice Cream

(6 servings)

A tropical treat; papaya might be used this way, too.

Whip in blender

1 cup heavy cream
¼ cup confectioners' sugar

Transfer to bowl. Purée in blender

2 ripe mangos, peeled (to make about 1½ cups purée)

Add

1 tablespoon lemon juice
1 cup macadamia nuts

Blend a few seconds to chop nuts. Combine mixture with whipped cream. Freeze until firm in tray or flat pan.

Oriental Marlow

(6 servings)

Spicy, smooth and unusual.

Whip in blender

> 1 cup heavy cream

Turn into bowl.

Place in blender container

> 1 cup milk
> Dash of salt
> ¼ cup orange marmalade
> ¼ cup preserved ginger
> ¼ cup nuts
> 16 marshmallows (¼ pound)

Blend these ingredients until solids are finely chopped. Fold in cream. Freeze in refrigerator tray at coldest temperature until firm.

Strawberry Ice Cream Roll

(8 to 10 servings)

Very pretty, very good.

Place in blender container

> 1-pound package frozen strawberries, thawed
> 1 cup light cream
> Juice of 1 lemon (about 3 tablespoons)
> ⅓ cup sugar

Blend until berries are fine. Pour into refrigerator tray and freeze. Meanwhile, crush in blender cookies or pound cake to make

> 1 cup cooky or cake crumbs

Whip in blender until stiff

> 1 cup heavy cream
> 2 tablespoons sugar
> ¼ teaspoon vanilla

Place a sheet of foil on a cooky sheet and spread cake or cooky crumbs on foil in a rectangle about 11 by 14 inches. Spread sweetened whipped cream over crumbs. Place in refrigerator to "set." When ice cream is frozen, make a mound of it across the width of the crumbs and cream. Working quickly, grasp edge of foil, lift and join edges of cream and crumbs around the ice cream. Place foil-wrapped roll in freezer and freeze until firm. Slice to serve. It's a good idea to remove roll from freezer 10 minutes before slicing. The strawberry center needs to warm up a little.

Fresh Strawberry Mousse

(6 servings)

The sherry flavor is optional.

Blender-whip and refrigerate

> 2 cups heavy cream

In blender container place

> 1 cup sugar
> 2 tablespoons plain gelatin
> ½ cup boiling water

Blend until gelatin is dissolved. Add gradually with motor running at low speed

> 1 quart fresh strawberries, stemmed
> ⅓ cup sherry, fruit juice or milk
> 1 dozen almond macaroons

When berries are puréed and macaroons crumbled fine, mix with whipped cream, turn into a large (or two small) refrigerator tray and freeze until firm. Cut in squares and garnish with a few sliced strawberries.

Watermelon Sherbet

(4 servings)

It's made by a special method for smooth texture.

Place in blender container

> 2 cups diced seeded watermelon
> 1 cup watermelon juice
> ½ cup sugar
> ¼ cup lemon juice

Blend until melon is liquefied. Freeze to a mush in refrigerator tray.

Boil until it spins a thread (230° to 238°)

> ½ cup sugar
> ⅓ cup water
> ¼ teaspoon salt

Cool slightly.

Beat until stiff

> 2 egg whites

Pour hot sirup slowly over egg whites, beating constantly until mixture piles and cools. Fold or stir into frozen melon mixture and freeze until firm. Stir several times during freezing.

PIE CRUSTS AND PIES

I haven't found it practical to make pie pastry in a blender. Much better results are to be had the regular way. But it's fun to grate cheese or grind nuts quickly in the blender to be rolled into pastry for certain pies—cheese for apple pie, nuts for a banana-cream pie, for instance.

Any pie filling that calls for chopped or puréed ingredients can be made in the blender—at least in part. Custard types, of which our friend pumpkin is an example, are very quickly put together this way.

Crumb Pie Crusts

Nothing will ever take the place of flaky pie pastry, of course; but for some pie fillings, especially the cream fillings and the fruit chiffon kind, crumb crusts are perfect. Graham Cracker Crust probably is most popular, but cooky crusts are delectable too. For a filling that holds its shape well, ground nuts can be used as the pie's foundation. For all of these crumb crusts, the blender was heaven sent.

Don't put too many crackers or cookies into the blender at once. Break 3 or 4 into the blender, crush them fine, turn them into a bowl and repeat the performance. A flash of the steel blades and the job is done each time.

Graham Cracker Crust

> 16 to 18 graham crackers, blender-crushed
> ½ cup melted butter
> 3 tablespoons sugar

Combine ingredients and pack firmly over bottom and sides of 9-inch pie pan. Chill until firm or bake for 8 minutes in a moderate oven, 350°. Then chill before adding filling.

Cooky Crumb Crust

> 1¼ cups blender-crushed cookies (vanilla or choco-
> late wafers or gingersnaps)
> ⅓ cup melted butter
> 1 tablespoon sugar

Combine crumbs, butter and sugar, and pack firmly over bottom and sides of 9-inch pie pan. Keep out a few crumbs to sprinkle over the top of the pie if you like. Chill this crust. Don't bake it. If you like, use crumbs just for the bottom of the pie and stand whole cookies up around the rim.

Corn Flake Crumb Crust

1¼ cups crushed corn flakes or wheat flakes (about
  4 cups whole flakes)
½ cup melted butter
⅓ cup sugar
½ teaspoon cinnamon (optional)

Combine ingredients and pack over bottom and sides of 9-inch pie pan. Chill before filling.

Nut Crust

1 cup blender-ground pecans, walnuts, black walnuts or Brazil nuts
3 tablespoons sugar

Combine and press over bottom and sides of pie plate. This crust clings to the pie, but doesn't hold its own shape very well. Delectable with any cream filling.

PIES YOU'LL ENJOY MAKING

Grated Apple Pie

(9-inch pie)

Super-delicious, and without a crust.

Place in blender container

2 egg yolks
⅓ cup sugar (more for apples not fully ripe)
2 tablespoons cornstarch
3 tablespoons butter
½ teaspoon each: cinnamon, nutmeg
½ cup cream

Blend just a second or two, then slice into the blender container with motor running

> 5 large juicy apples

When apples have been cut fine, fill buttered pie plate without a pastry lining. The pie holds shape without a crust. Bake at 350° for 25 minutes. Beat until stiff, using hand beater

> 2 egg whites
> ½ teaspoon lemon extract

Beat in, until mixture stands in peaks

> ¼ cup sugar

Spread this meringue on pie and brown in moderate oven, 350°, about 15 minutes.

Apple Turnovers

(Makes 8)

An old-fashioned treat.

Chop in blender container

> 2 large or 3 medium-sized cored apples, ·cut into eighths (for best results chop each apple separately, emptying container after each one)

To chopped apples add

> ½ cup plumped raisins
> 3 tablespoons sugar
> ¼ teaspoon cinnamon
> Dash salt

Prepare

> 1 recipe plain pastry (your own or a packaged one)

Roll pastry ⅛ inch thick, then cut into 4-inch squares. Place a large tablespoonful of apple mixture and ½ teaspoon butter in center of each square. Dampen edges with water, then fold each square from corner to corner to form a triangle. Crimp edges together with a well-floured fork and prick top of each turnover to let steam escape. Place on cooky sheet and bake in hot oven, 450°, for 20 to 25 minutes or until brown.

Heavenly Cherry Pie

(9-inch pie; 6 cuts)

Snow white, and rose red!

Soften in ¼ cup cold water and then dissolve over hot water

> 1 tablespoon plain gelatin

Cook without stirring to 240°

> ½ cup sugar
> ⅓ cup water

Meanwhile, whip until stiff

> 2 egg whites
> ⅛ teaspoon salt

While beating, add gradually the hot sirup, then the dissolved gelatin. Keep beating continuously with electric mixer or rotary beater, until all sirup and gelatin have been well mixed. Add

> 1 tablespoon lemon juice
> 1 cup heavy cream, whipped in blender

Spread fluffy white mixture in

> Baked 9-inch pie shell

Chill.

Purée in blender

> Drained cherries from 1-pound can
> Few drops red food color

Add and blend a few seconds

½ cup sugar
2½ tablespoons cornstarch
¼ cup cherry liqueur (such as Cherry Heering)

Turn blended mixture into saucepan, cook and stir until thickened and clear. Cool and spread over filling in pie shell. Chill again for several hours before serving.

Coconut Cream Pie

(9-inch pie)

Coconut flavor but no shreds.

Place in blender container

1 cup milk
3 eggs
1 cup coconut
¼ teaspoon salt
3 tablespoons cornstarch
3 tablespoons flour
⅔ cup sugar

Blend about 20 seconds and pour into saucepan, adding

1 cup more milk

Cook, stirring constantly, over moderate heat until filling is thickened and quite stiff. Keep stirring or you may scorch the mixture. Remove from heat and add

1 teaspoon vanilla
2 tablespoons butter

Cool and spread in baked pie shell or Chocolate-Cooky crust (see p. 139). Chill and top with

1 cup heavy cream, blender-whipped

Chocolate Cream Pie

Use the preceding recipe but substitute 2 squares chocolate, melted, for the coconut. Replace a cup of milk with a cup of strong coffee for mocha pie with chocolate.

Date Custard Pie

(9-incher; 6 cuts)

A simple dessert.

Place in blender

> 1 cup pitted dates (8 ounces)
> ½ cup sugar
> 1 cup hot milk

Blend until smooth and add

> 1¼ cups more milk
> 2 eggs
> Dash of salt
> Dash of nutmeg

Blend a few seconds and pour into

> Pastry-lined pie pan

Bake in hot oven, 450°, for 10 minutes; reduce heat to 350° for 25 minutes longer.

Frozen Lemon Pie

(9-inch pie)

Four eggs, half a lemon.

Place in blender and blend until dissolved

> ½ cup hot water
> 1 tablespoon plain gelatin
> ½ cup sugar

Add

> 4 egg yolks
> ½ large lemon, seeded, cut in pieces (use all outer peel, but remove most of white part)

Blend smooth. Chill until thick, not stiff. Fold together

4 egg whites, beaten stiff
½ cup sugar

Fold meringue into thickened lemon custard, turn into crumb crust or baked shell and freeze until firm. Makes a good pudding minus crust, without freezing.

Nut Slices

(16 servings)

Flaky pastry with a rich filling.

Pastry:

Place in blender

1 cup very soft butter
1 egg
¼ cup sour cream

Blend thoroughly. Stir into

2 cups sifted flour

Shape into 2 balls, wrap in wax paper and chill while preparing the filling.

Filling:

Place in blender

4 egg yolks
⅔ cup sugar
1 teaspoon vanilla
¼ teaspoon salt

Mix until thick and lemon colored. Add

1 cup walnuts

Blend until nuts are ground fine. Fold this mixture into

4 egg whites, stiffly beaten

Roll each ball of dough on a pastry cloth into a rectangle about 9 by 13 inches. Place one piece in pan the same size.

Spread evenly with filling. Top with remaining pastry. Bake at 375° for 35 minutes. Cut into bars while warm.

Orange Coconut Pie

(9-inch pie)

A real palate pleaser.

Place in blender container and blend until dissolved

> 1 tablespoon plain gelatin in
> ½ cup hot milk

Add

> ¾ cup more milk
> ½ cup orange juice
> Pared outer rind from ½ orange
> 1 strip (about an inch square) lemon rind
> 2 tablespoons lemon juice
> ¼ teaspoon salt
> ⅓ cup sugar
> 2 egg yolks

Blend until rinds are cut fine, turn into saucepan and cook over low heat, stirring constantly, until custardy. It is really better to do this in the top of a double boiler over hot water, in order not to overcook eggs. Cool, then chill until slightly thickened. Fold in

> 2 egg whites, beaten stiff, then beaten with
> ¼ cup sugar

Pour into

> Baked pie shell or graham-cracker crust

Sprinkle with

> ⅓ cup shredded coconut

Chill until firm.

Chilled Pineapple Cottage Cheese Pie

(6 servings)

Light-textured and appealing.

Place in blender container

> ⅓ cup sugar
> 1½ tablespoons plain gelatin
> ½ cup boiling water

Blend to dissolve sugar and gelatin. Cool somewhat and add

> 1 cup cottage cheese
> 2 tablespoons lemon juice
> 1 teaspoon nutmeg
> ¼ teaspoon salt
> ¼ teaspoon vanilla
> 1 cup crushed pineapple with juice

Blend smooth. Turn into bowl and chill until slightly thickened. Meanwhile rinse blender, dry and place in it

> 1 cup heavy cream

Whip the cream and fold it into pineapple-cheese mixture. Turn into

> Graham Cracker Crust, page 139

Chill until firm.

Fluffy Prune Pie

(9-inch pie)

Rich stuff, so cut the pieces small!

Place in blender container

> ¼ cup orange juice
> 1 small piece lemon rind (outer peel)
> 1 teaspoon lemon juice

Blend until rind is grated. Without stopping blender add gradually

>1 pound of pitted prunes, cooked until very soft

Blend smooth. Add

>1 cup walnuts or pecans

Blend a few seconds to chop. Pour into mixing bowl and mix in

>¾ cup sugar
>¼ teaspoon salt

Beat until stiff, then fold in

>2 egg whites

Pour into baked 9-inch pie shell and bake at 325° for 30 minutes. When cool top with whipped cream to which you have added 2 drops almond extract. Pie is rich and sweet, so I prefer not to sweeten whipped cream for it.

Pumpkin Pie

(9-inch pie; 6 cuts)

Try squash in the same recipe.

>1½ cups cooked or canned pumpkin
>1½ cups milk or milk and cream or evaporated milk
>3 eggs
>¾ cup brown or white sugar
>¼ teaspoon salt
>1 teaspoon cinnamon
>1 teaspoon nutmeg
>½ teaspoon ginger

Place your hand on the blender cover before starting the motor. Blend just a few seconds, until smooth, and pour into pastry-lined pie shell. Bake at 450° for 10 minutes, then bake at 350° for 30 minutes longer, or until firm in the center. A piece of outer peel of orange can be blender-grated into the pie. Add with ½ cup milk at the beginning and blend fine before adding other ingredients.

Sour Cream Raisin Pie

(8-inch pie; 5 cuts)

Easiest of raisin pies, and one of the best.

> 1 cup sour cream
> 2 eggs
> 1 cup seeded raisins
> ¼ teaspoon salt
> ½ teaspoon nutmeg
> 1 teaspoon cinnamon
> 1 teaspoon cornstarch
> ⅔ cup sugar

Blend a minute or two or until raisins are well chopped. Pour into a baked 8-inch pie shell. Bake at 450° for 10 minutes, then bake at 325° for 25 minutes more. Cool and serve with whipped-cream topping.

Strawberry Devonshire Pie

(9-inch pie; serves 6)

Pretty as a color photograph and tastier than that!

Place in blender container

> 1 tablespoon plain gelatin
> ¼ cup hot water
> ¼ cup sugar

Blend a few seconds and add

> 3 tablespoons lemon juice
> ¼ teaspoon salt
> 4 egg yolks

Blend a few seconds and turn into a saucepan. Cook over hot water or very low heat until custard thickens. Cool.

Meanwhile whirl until smooth in blender

>1 cup cottage cheese

Add to gelatin mixture and chill until it begins to thicken. Whip until soft peaks form

>4 egg whites

Gradually beat in

>½ cup sugar

Beat until meringue holds stiff peaks. Fold into gelatin mixture. Fold in also

>1 pint sliced strawberries

Pour into

>Baked 9-inch pie shell

Chill until firm.

Taffy Pie

(8-inch pie; 6 servings)

Something like pecan pie—luscious!

Place in blender container

>2 eggs
>2 teaspoons water
>1 tablespoon melted butter
>2 teaspoons vanilla
>1½ cups dark brown sugar

Blend a few seconds to mix well. Add and blend until chopped

>1 cup pecans

Pour into

>Gingersnap pie crust, page 139

Bake at 350° for 30 minutes or until firm.

6 | Drinks

Drinks are what blenders were invented for. The Frozen Daiquiri that comes out of the container the consistency of a sherbet, the thick foamy Chocolate Malted Milk, the Mocha Mint Cooler with its fresh mint blended right in are beverages you can prepare in no other way. How else can you make a drink of pineapple juice and *liquid* carrot?

Fruits and fruit juices, milk and eggs, even vegetables, can be made into countless wonderful drinks. In this harried, hurried age many people are drinking their breakfasts which can be nutritious and adequate—egg, juice and milk, all in one. I don't recommend this as a regular practice, but where speed counts more than family togetherness it has merit.

Cocktails and Drinks Made with Liquor and Wine

This group of recipes represents many of the blender-made favorites in homes and at famous bars. There are some "ladies' drinks" among them—so called because they are pretty and delicious from the first sip—since the blender is perfect for mixing any drink that's frothy, fluffy or fruited.

You can make any drink better in a blender if it's a drink that needs shaking or vigorous mixing. If the recipe says "Shake with ice," give it a whirl in the blender, and it will be better than you've ever had it.

How Long Do You Blend a Drink?

Only a few seconds for most drinks. Just on, off and pour. Drinks of the daiquiri type which you want frozen or semi-frozen may take a minute. Malted milks thin down if over-blended. You'll rapidly catch on to how long it takes in the kind of machine you have.

How Much Ice Do You Use?

A rule of thumb: about ½ cup cracked ice per drink (alcoholic); twice as much if you want it frozen. When you make as many as 4 drinks at once you don't need ½ cup ice for each; 1 cup usually is enough for four. The amount of ice is really a matter of personal preference. A lot dilutes your drink, but maybe you want it diluted!

It is better to crack or crush ice before putting it into the blender. Whole ice cubes may dull the cutting edges of the blender blades. Use an ice crusher or a canvas bag and mallet or hammer. Some blender manufacturers say that it's O.K. to crush ice in small amounts if you use a cup of water in the container.

Bartender's Ballad: "An extra chill is an extra thrill."

Fill your glasses with cracked ice while they wait to be filled.

Chill your blender container and ingredients.

Table of Equivalents

1 jigger = 1½ ounces, or 3 tablespoons
1 pony = 1 ounce, or 2 tablespoons
juice of 1 lemon = about 3 tablespoons
juice of 1 lime = about 1½ tablespoons
dash = about ⅛ teaspoon
4 ounces = ½ cup or 8 tablespoons

SUGAR in blender drinks: You get perfect solution whether you use granulated, bar sugar or a sirup. Rule of thumb about sugar and lemon: 1 jigger of lemon juice calls for 1 teaspoon of sugar to sweeten.

THE ALEXANDER FAMILY

Alexanders are after-dinner drinks. Never serve them before a meal. They're too rich and sweet. Chill the ingredients first if you have time.

Alexander

(4 drinks)

Tastes so good!

> 4 ounces gin
> 4 ounces whipping cream
> 4 ounces crème de cacao
> About 1 cup cracked ice

Switch motor on for just a few seconds, then off. Strain.

Brandy Alexander

Substitute brandy for gin.

Alexander's Southern Cousin

Substitute Southern Comfort for gin. This one's perfection!

Alexander's Sister

(4 drinks)

See the resemblance?

> 4 ounces gin
> 4 ounces whipping cream

4 ounces crème de menthe
About 1 cup cracked ice

Blend for a few seconds and strain out ice.

Pump Room Alexander

(4 drinks)

Gets a fourth partner!

3 ounces gin (or brandy)
3 ounces whipping cream
3 ounces crème de cacao
3 ounces crème de menthe
1 cup or more cracked ice

Blend a few seconds; strain out ice.

Bud's Special

(2 drinks)

A shirttail relative.

4 ounces Cointreau
2 ounces heavy cream
Dash of angostura bitters
About 1 cup cracked ice

Switch on the motor for about 6 seconds; then off, and strain.

Grasshopper

(4 drinks)

An attractive, popular young cousin.

4 ounces white crème de cacao
4 ounces green crème de menthe
4 ounces whipping cream
About 1 cup cracked ice

Switch on motor for a few seconds; then off, and strain. Brown crème de cacao was originally used in this drink, but while taste was divine, the color was bad.

Pink Elephant

Strangely, this is a Grasshopper made with pink crème de menthe! White crème de cacao is a must in this case.

THE COLLINSES

These are the tall refreshers, the lemonades with a built-in relaxer. They're for the hot days of summer and sipping through straws. Put ice cubes in your tallest glasses for them.

Tom Collins

(1 drink)

Most gregarious of the Collins boys!

>1 jigger lemon juice (lime is good, too)
>1 jigger gin
>1 teaspoon sugar
>½ cup cracked ice

Give these ingredients a quick whirl in your blender, and pour over 2 or 3 ice cubes in a tall glass (10- or 12-ounce). Add a cherry, and fill glass with seltzer. A mint-leaf garnish is pretty.

John Collins

Same thing, only with whisky instead of gin.

Mint Collins with Fresh Mint

Put 2 or 3 mint leaves into the blender with any collins.

DAIQUIRIS

Most people like daiquiris to be of a slushy consistency—which takes 5 to 8 ounces cracked ice for one—but with more ice it is possible to serve them really sherbeted. Use sherbet glasses, if you haven't big champagne glasses, and short straws.

If you don't want your daiquiri frozen, don't blend it more than just a few seconds.

Chill the blender and the rum.

In the second recipe, Frozen Daiquiri to keep on hand, the mixture is frozen to begin with. Therefore it requires only a few seconds to "fluff it up."

Frozen Daiquiri

(1 drink)

World famous, and no wonder.

> 1 jigger light rum
> Juice ½ lime (1 if small and not very juicy)
> 1 teaspoon sugar
> 1 cup crushed ice

Blend ingredients until you have the texture you want.

Frozen Daiquiri (to Keep on Hand)

(About 8 drinks)

A pungent sherbet!

> 1 can frozen concentrate for limeade
> 2 canfuls (juice cans) light rum
> 3 canfuls water

Mix ingredients and freeze. When you wish to make daiquiris, spoon some of the mixture into your blender, give it a quick whirl and turn it out sherbeted into champagne glasses of the saucer type, or sherbet dishes. Garnish each drink with a mint leaf if you can. Serve with a straw in each.

Frozen Whisky Sour

(About 8 drinks)

Have a company drink at any time!

> 1 can lemonade concentrate
> 2 canfuls bourbon
> 3 canfuls water
> 1 tablespoon frozen orange juice concentrate

Mix, freeze and store until you want one. Spoon some of the mixture into your blender, switch on and off and serve it sherbeted in champagne saucers or sherbet glasses, with straws and mint-leaf garnish.

The larger, 12-ounce cans of concentrate will give you twice the amount, using the same ratio of other ingredients. True of the Frozen Daiquiri, also.

Mint Daiquiri

Just put a couple of fresh mint leaves into the blender with each daiquiri. You couldn't make this one without a blender, and it's delightful.

Frozen Fruit Daiquiri

(Makes 6)

Some drinks are merely wonderful, but some are oo-oo wonderful! This one is!

> 1 cup light rum
> Juice of 3 limes
> 1 box (12 ounces) frozen peaches (or berries or
>   pineapple)
> 2 cups crushed ice

Blend this mixture (break up fruit slightly first) a minute or so, until it is nice and slushy. This could be your dessert! An utterly luxurious touch may be achieved by adding a jigger of Grand Marnier to this lovely concoction.

Bacardi Cocktail

(2 drinks)

Daiquiri with grenadine, a pretty pink.

> 2 jiggers Bacardi rum
> Juice of 2 limes
> 1 jigger grenadine
> 1 cup (or more) cracked ice

Blend it short to sip from the glass; longer and with more ice to frappé it and drink with straws.

Cuban Special

(For 2)

Really delightful!

> 2 jiggers light rum
> Juice 1 lime
> 2 jiggers fresh or frozen pineapple juice
> 2 teaspoons apricot brandy
> 1 cup (or more) cracked ice

Blend 1 minute or more, to the consistency you like. To get fresh pineapple juice, all you have to do is blend cut-up fresh pineapple!

Frosted Pineapple

(For 2)

Almost a daiquiri, and one of the most delectable drinks ever invented!

2 jiggers light rum
3 slices fresh, very ripe pineapple, pared, cored,
    cut up
1 tablespoon sugar
2 cups cracked ice

Blend to a slushy consistency. Garnish with mint, or blend with two sprigs of mint. Leave out the rum and it's still good!

THE MILKY WAY—A Collection of Drinks
Made with Milk, Eggs and Liquors

When you double a recipe calling for 1 egg or 1 egg white for 1 drink, you don't always use 2 eggs or 2 whites for 2 drinks. In most cases 1 egg will do for 2 drinks as well as for one.

Don't prolong the blending of a drink containing milk or egg or you'll get too much foam. Some foam is very nice, but nobody wants to acquire a white mustache drinking through the bubbles.

Eggnog

(1 drink)

New Year's cheer, but good any time.

1 jigger rum, brandy, whisky or sherry
5 ounces milk or milk and cream
1 egg
1 teaspoon sugar
2 ice cubes, cracked

Blend just a few seconds, strain into glass and top with nutmeg. One of the best of all eggnogs is the preceding, made with ½ rum, ½ brandy.

Hot Eggnog

For whed your doze is stobbed ub—or for any cold day.

Use the preceding recipe, minus ice. Rinse out the blender

container with hot water, put in egg and give it a quick whirl. Then gradually add combination of milk, sugar and liquor heated just to the boiling point, no further. Blend about 2 seconds and serve at once in preheated mugs.

Banana Cow

(1 tall glass or 2 small ones)

This one's good. Skip the rum and you can give it to the kiddies.

> 1 ripe banana, cut in pieces
> 1 tablespoon sugar
> 3 ounces milk
> 1 jigger light rum
> 1 cup cracked ice

Blend a few seconds to liquefy the banana before you add ice. Then give it another quick whirl and strain out the ice.

And—Oh Goody!—Ice Cream!

You can use vanilla ice cream instead of whipping cream in any drink like the Alexander, or try one of these bright ideas.

Crème de Café

(Fills 8 champagne glasses)

More than slightly sensational!

> 1 cup bourbon
> 1 cup cold water
> 1 tablespoon instant coffee
> 1 pint vanilla ice cream

Just on and off with the blender switch.

Cricket

(For 2)

Reminds you of an Alexander.

> 2 jiggers crème de cacao
> 1 jigger brandy
> 1 scoop vanilla ice cream

Switch on, switch off.

Golden Gate

(For 2)

Not bad!

> 2 jiggers gin or light rum
> ½ pint orange ice or sherbet

Blend smooth. With vanilla ice cream you'd call the drink "White Cargo."

Kiss o' the Nile

(4 drinks)

A warm-day refresher.

> ½ pint lemon-lime sherbet
> 2 jiggers gin
> ½ cup crushed ice

Whirl to a froth and serve in cocktail glasses. Get the best sherbet you can buy, for this drink is all taste. Add a mint leaf to each serving.

Fizzes, Flips and Eggish Drinks

Remember, don't overblend, or you'll be burying your nose in bubbles to get to the drink!

Bacardi Flip (Rum Flip)

(4 drinks)

This one's good 2 ways.

> 3 eggs
> 4 jiggers Bacardi rum
> 4 teaspoons sugar
> Dash angostura bitters
> 1 cup cracked ice

Blend just a few seconds; strain. Add a twist of outer rind of lemon to each serving. Or you may skip the bitters and lemon and sprinkle the drink with nutmeg.

Cherry Flip

(2 drinks)

Delicious!

> 1 egg
> 6 ounces Danish cherry wine
> 2 teaspoons sugar
> 1 tablespoon lemon juice
> ½ cup cracked ice

Blend and leave the ice in.

Claret Flip

(For 2)

Dusty pink, and very nice.

> 1 egg
> 6 ounces claret, Burgundy or cabernet
> 1 tablespoon sugar
> ½ cup cracked ice

Blend about 10 seconds and leave ice in. Sprinkle with nutmeg or add a dash of bitters.

Port or Sherry Flip

Same thing, only with a sweeter wine you can cut the sugar down to a teaspoonful for 2 drinks, or skip it altogether.

Clover Club

(For 2)

Frequent feminine choice.

> 2 jiggers gin
> 1 jigger grenadine
> 3 tablespoons lemon or lime juice
> 1 egg white
> 1 cup cracked ice

Blend a few seconds; strain or not. For a less sweet drink cut down the grenadine slightly.

Clover Leaf

This is a Clover Club floating a mint leaf, or better, a nice clean clover leaf from your back yard.

Coffee with Kirsch Cocktail (Café au Kirsch)

(For 2)

Better after dinner.

> 2 ounces kirsch (or ½ kirsch, ½ cognac)
> ¼ cup cold water
> 1 teaspoon instant coffee
> 1 egg white
> 1½ teaspoons sugar
> 1 cup cracked ice

Blend a few seconds and strain or not.

Use freshly brewed instant espresso coffee for this drink when you can.

Coffee Cocktail

(For 2)

There's no coffee in it, but it looks and tastes surprisingly coffeeish.

> 2 ounces port
> 2 ounces rum or brandy
> 1 egg
> 1 teaspoon sugar
> 1 cup cracked ice

Switch on the motor; switch it off. Strain or not.

Green Elevator (Chartreuse Cocktail)

(2 drinks)

Unusual and most delicious!

> 2 jiggers green chartreuse
> Juice 1 lemon
> 2 tablespoons grapefruit juice
> 1 egg white
> 1 cup cracked ice

Blend a few seconds; strain out ice. Warning: chartreuse is expensive!

Morning Glory

(For 2)

A green flower.

> 2 jiggers gin
> Juice of 1 lime
> 1 egg

4 teaspoons green crème de menthe
1 cup cracked ice

Blend a few seconds and strain or not.

Pink Cloud

(4 drinks)

Pinkly pretty!

4 ounces gin
4 ounces pineapple juice
2 ounces grenadine
1 egg white
2 cups cracked ice

Blend in a whirl and leave the ice in.

Pink Lady

(2 drinks)

Such a charming girl!

1 jigger gin
1 tablespoon apple brandy
1 tablespoon lemon juice
1 tablespoon grenadine sirup
1 egg white
½ cup cracked ice

Blend about 10 seconds and leave ice in drink.

Ramos Gin Fizz

(For 2)

Justly famous.

1 jigger lemon juice, or ½ lemon, ½ lime juice
1 teaspoon sugar
2 jiggers gin
1 egg white

2 jiggers cream
About 10 drops orange flower water (from drug-
store)
½ to 1 cup cracked ice

Blend a few seconds. Some recipes direct you to fill the glass with club soda. We didn't. Advice from a prominent bar manager: "Coat" the glass with the orange flower water. Let it run around inside as you turn the glass, pour out any excess and add your drink. This way you'd probably use more than the 10 drops suggested.

Rum Fizz

(For 2)

Fruited and frothy.

2 jiggers rum
2 ounces lemon juice
2 teaspoons sugar
1 egg or 1 egg white
1 slice canned pineapple, cut up
1 cup cracked ice

Blend a few seconds; leave ice in.

Shamrock

(For 2)

Green as the auld sod.

2 jiggers gin
Juice 2 small limes
2 tablespoons green crème de menthe
1 egg white
1 cup or more cracked ice

Blend long enough to get a sherbety consistency; give it the consistency of a Frozen Daiquiri. You may have to add more ice. If you can find fresh clover leaves, use them for garnish.

Silver Fizz

(Individual drink)

Tall and pale.

> 1 jigger gin (or use rum if you'd rather)
> Juice ½ lemon
> 1 teaspoon sugar
> 1 egg white
> ½ cup cracked ice

Blend, leaving the ice in. Pour into 8-ounce glass and fill with sparkling water. Nice summer drink, especially as an afternoon pickup.

Sloe Gin Fizz

(For 2)

Pretty, like pink lemonade.

> Juice 1 lemon
> 2 teaspoons sugar
> 2 jiggers sloe gin
> ½ cup cracked ice

Blend a few seconds, pour into 8-ounce glasses and fill with carbonated water. Made the same way, only with gin, it's a Gin Fizz.

A BOUQUET OF ROSES

Rose Blossom

(8 drinks)

A summer beauty.

> 1 can (6 ounces) frozen lemonade concentrate
> 1½ cups rosé wine
> 1 cup crushed ice*

Blend until ice is liquefied.

*With this amount of liquid it is all right to use ice cubes—four of them—instead of crushed ice.

La Vie en Rose

(For 2)

Such a lovely rose!

> ½ jigger lemon juice
> ½ jigger grenadine
> 1 jigger gin
> 1 jigger kirsch
> ½ cup cracked ice

Blend just a second or two and strain.

Jack Rose

(For 2)

How'd that man get in here?

> 1 ounce lime or lemon juice
> 2 jiggers applejack brandy
> 2 tablespoons grenadine sirup
> 1 egg white (not a necessary ingredient, but makes
>   it smoother)
> ½ cup cracked ice

Switch on, switch off and strain.

Rose in June

(1 drink)

But good in January, too.

> Juice 1 orange
> Juice 2 small limes

1 jigger raspberry sirup
1 jigger gin
½ cup cracked ice

Blend quickly and leave ice in drink.

Rosemary

(4 drinks)

Feminine in name only; a good appetizer.

1 jigger cherry brandy
1 jigger French vermouth
2 jiggers gin
½ cup cracked ice

Blend a second or two and strain. Garnish with a cherry for each.

Rose Petal

(4 drinks)

Garnish with a rose petal if you can—lovely!

½ pint raspberry sherbet
1 jigger cognac
1 jigger white crème de cacao
½ cup crushed ice

Blend a few seconds and pour into glasses.

ADDED ATTRACTIONS—Some Famous Cocktails and a Few Exotic Beverages

Bronx Cocktail

(For 2)

Excellent before-dinner drink.

>1 jigger orange juice
>1 jigger dry vermouth
>1 jigger sweet vermouth
>1 jigger gin
>1 cup cracked ice

Turn the switch, say "I'll have a Bronx, please," turn off the blender and strain or not.

Champêche

(For 2)

To toast a bride!

>1 fresh peach, cut in pieces, lightly sugared
>10 ounces chilled champagne

Whirl peach to a liquid in blender, turn into 2 of your best crystal goblets and add champagne. Some cracked ice in the drink is advisable. Use frozen peaches, if you wish.

Cherry Blossom

(For 2)

Like pink lemonade!

>2 jiggers sloe gin
>1 ounce orange juice
>1 tablespoon lemon juice
>1 tablespoon maraschino cherry juice or
>   cherry liqueur
>1 cup cracked ice

Blend a few seconds and strain or leave ice in. This is pretty and can be frappéed if you'll double the ice and blend longer.

Cotton Picker Cocktail

(For 2)

A good afternoon pick-me-up.

2 ounces Southern Comfort
2 ounces orange juice
1 ounce rum
1 ounce lemon juice
1 cup cracked ice

Blend, strain or not. More ice will frappé this drink, and that's nice, too. If you frappé it, serve it with straws, of course.

Crème de Menthe Frappé

Convert cracked ice to shaved ice in your blender, pack your glasses with that and pour crème de menthe over the ice to fill the glass. Naturally, use straws. Try this also with crème de cacao, curaçao, Grand Marnier or any liqueur that tastes good by itself.

Hawaiian Punch

(2 drinks)

Very exotic, especially if it is served in a coconut.

3 ounces gin or light rum
3 ounces coconut milk
1 jigger lemon juice
1 teaspoon curaçao or Grand Marnier
2 teaspoons sugar
About 2 cups cracked ice

Blend until sherbety. If you want to be *very* fancy, bore a largish hole in one of the coconut eyes, after draining the milk and making the drink, and use a small funnel to put the drink into the coconut, from which it can be sipped through straws!

Honolulu Wine Cooler

(4 sizable drinks)

Oh, so refreshing!

1 cup fresh or canned pineapple, cut up
6 ounces any dry white wine
6 ounces sherry
Juice ½ lemon
1½ cups cracked ice

Blend until pineapple is liquefied, and leave ice in drink. This almost makes the capacity of the blender container, so keep your hand on the blender top when starting the motor—you don't want a splashover!

Mint Cocktail

(For 2)

Real mint flavor and a pretty color.

2 sprigs fresh mint
2 jiggers any dry white wine
1½ jiggers gin
½ jigger crème de menthe
½ to 1 cup cracked ice

Blend about 20 seconds. Do not strain.

Orange Blossom

(For 2)

A lovely refresher.

2 jiggers gin (or rum)
2 jiggers orange juice
1 tablespoon lemon juice
1 teaspoon sugar
½ cup (or more) cracked ice
2 slices orange

Blend all but orange slices for a few seconds, or use more ice and blend to sherbet consistency. Float thin orange slice on drink or hang half orange slice over edge of glass.

Pineapple Cooler

(For 2)

There's something about fresh pineapple!

> 2 jiggers gin
> 2 slices fresh pineapple, cut in pieces
> 1 ounce green crème de menthe
> 1 cup cracked ice

Blend until smooth and leave ice in.

Planter's Punch

(For 2)

A man's drink.

> 1 jigger orange juice
> 1 jigger pineapple juice
> 2 ounces lime or lemon juice
> 2 teaspoons sugar or grenadine
> 4 ounces Jamaica rum
> 1 cup cracked ice

Blend quickly and serve with ice left in and more ice in the glass. Garnish with fruit—a half slice of orange and a cherry —and add a sprig of mint.

Poinciana

(For 4)

Richly fruited.

> 4 jiggers light rum
> 4 maraschino cherries
> 2 slices whole orange
> 2 jiggers apple juice
> 1 jigger grenadine

Blend 30 seconds or until fruit is liquefied. Strain into glasses half filled with cracked ice.

Frozen Scotch

(1 drink)

Make it bourbon if you'd rather.

> 1 jigger Scotch
> 1 jigger lemon juice
> 1 teaspoon sugar
> About 1½ cups cracked ice

Blend to a sherbet consistency and serve in an Old Fashioned glass.

Splendito

(4 servings)

How to begin a party for ladies.

> 14 to 16 minted pineapple chunks
> 1 teaspoon sugar
> ½ ounce Cointreau
> 3 ounces light rum
> Cracked ice
> Maraschino cherries

Combine pineapple, sugar, liqueur, rum and about ½ cup ice in blender. Whirl a few seconds and serve over more ice. Garnish each serving with a cherry and 2 minted pineapple chunks speared on a cocktail pick. Add colored straws.

Stinger

(For 2)

A popular after-dinner drink.

1 jigger brandy
1 jigger white crème de menthe
½ cup cracked ice

On, off and strain. There are several special versions of this drink. Half an egg white may be added for 2 drinks. Stingers also can be nicely frosted. Increase the ice and blend until you get sherbet consistency. This requires straws, of course.

MORE DRINKS, THE NONALCOHOLIC KIND

Your blender will make cabbage or carrot juice for you, liquefy any fruit or vegetable—nuts, coconuts, dates and figs. It will even make drinkable the core of an apple or the shell of an egg. Maybe you want to drink these—I don't. But a blender can make it possible to drink them.

How to Liquefy a Solid in the Blender

Pour water, milk or fruit juice into the blender container until the blades are covered. Add the solid in pieces, a few at a time (for example: 1 carrot, cut up, or 1 apple, sliced). Cover the container and put your hand lightly on top. Turn the switch and blend first at low speed if your machine has several speeds. Then turn to high speed and run the motor until the food is drinkable. You can add more liquid to thin it if necessary. In general, it takes 2 parts of liquid to 1 of solid to make something you can drink.

Have Ingredients Cold, and Crack the Ice

Drinks made without ice, like the various milk drinks, need to be cold to begin with. Ice should be cracked. Some blenders will crush ice cubes in a cup or more of liquid, but as a rule it is much better to use cracked ice, for the sake of protecting the edges of the blender blades and as a precaution against breaking the glass container.

FRUIT AND VEGETABLE JUICE DRINKS

Fresh Apple Cocktail

(For 2)

One of the best of all; the fresh apple flavor is wonderful!

¼ cup water
1 tablespoon lemon juice
1 teaspoon sugar
1 sizable eating apple, cored and cut up (don't pare it)
½ cup cracked ice

Blend until the apple is liquefied. You may need to vary the lemon juice and sugar, depending on the kind of apples you use. Crisp fall apples like Jonathans, McIntoshes, Baldwins are good. Early apples may take more sugar, late apples more lemon juice.

Carrot and Pineapple Cocktail

(4 servings)

A good appetizer.

1½ cups pineapple juice
2 medium-sized carrots, cut in pieces
1 tablespoon lemon juice or 1 thick slice pared lemon

Have ingredients cold so that you needn't add ice. Blend until carrot is thoroughly liquefied. This looks good and tastes good. You can add ½ banana, a small cored and cut-up apple, or about ¼ bunch of watercress to make cocktails of varying flavors.

Carrot Milk

(2 or more drinks)

Good for the small fry!

>1 cup milk
>2 medium-sized carrots, cut in pieces

Blend until liquefied. This drink has an attractive pale-carrot tint and a coconut flavor, which is rather surprising.

Cherry Freeze

(For 3)

Warm-afternoon refresher.

>2 cups canned cherry juice
>1 tablespoon lemon juice
>2 scoops vanilla ice cream

Blend until smooth. Fill the tall glasses with sparkling water.

Cranberry Cocktail

(4 servings)

One of the best of appeteasers.

>2 cups raw cranberries
>1 cup water
>1 cup orange juice
>½ cup sugar
>Dash of salt

Blend until liquefied, strain and chill before serving.

Grapefruit Flip

(2 drinks in champagne or sherbet glasses)

Nice for the teetotalers at a cocktail party.

¾ cup grapefruit juice
2 tablespoons lemon juice
1 tablespoon grenadine sirup
1 egg white
½ cup cracked ice

Blend until frothy; don't overdo it.

Love Apple Cocktail

(4 servings)

First course at dinner.

1½ cups tomato juice
½ cup evaporated milk
¼ teaspoon celery salt
¼ teaspoon salt
Dash black pepper
½ cup cracked ice

Blend untli smooth and frothy.

Melon Cocktail

(For 2)

So delicious!

1 cup pineapple juice
1 cup diced cantaloupe, honeydew or other melon
1 tablespoon lemon juice

Have ingredients very cold and blend until melon is liquefied.
Garnish with mint.

Watermelon Juice

You can drink your watermelon if you remove the seeds and let the blender convert the melon to liquid. No juice or water needed. This is a delicious pink drink—pure watermelon.

Orange Flip

(4 servings)

Drink your breakfast!

> 1 can frozen orange juice
> 2¼ cups water
> 2 or 3 eggs
> 2 tablespoons sugar
> Dash salt

Blend 20 seconds or so. These are tall glasses.

Orange Frosted

(4 to 6 servings)

A wonderful trick with frozen juice.

> 1 can frozen orange juice
> 2¼ cups water
> 1 pint vanilla ice cream or pineapple sherbet

Blend 30 seconds to a minute. Serve in tall glasses.

Pineapple Drink

(For 2)

Oh, so good and refreshing!

> ¼ cup water or orange juice
> 2 cups diced fresh pineapple

  2 tablespoons sugar
  1 cup cracked ice

Blend to a smooth liquid. Then there's a fresh pineapple freeze made by adding a couple of scoops of ice cream to this.

Pineapple Fizz

(4 servings)

Frothy, white and pleasant.

  1 cup pineapple juice
  1 tablespoon lemon juice
  1 egg white
  Dash worcestershire sauce or bitters
  1 cup cracked ice

Blend and pour into tall glasses. Fill with sparkling water or ginger ale.

Pineapple Mint Freeze

(1 drink)

Smooth perfection!

  2 to 4 sprigs fresh mint
  1 cup pineapple juice
  1 scoop lemon sherbet

Blend until thick and smooth.

Pineapple Smash

(1 glass)

You can do this with any fruit juice.

  1 cup pineapple juice
  1 banana, in pieces
  ½ cup cracked ice

Blend until banana is liquefied.

Pineapple Watercress Cocktail

(4 or more appetizer drinks)

Lovely green, and DEE-licious!

> 2 cups pineapple juice
> 1 bunch watercress, washed, of course
> 3 tablespoons sugar
> 1 thick slice peeled lemon or
> 2 tablespoons lemon juice
> 1 cup cracked ice

Blend until cress becomes drinkable.

Raspberry Punch

(12 or more servings)

Or use loganberry or cherry juice.

> 1½ cups raspberry juice
> ½ cup lemon juice
> 1 cup orange juice
> ½ cup sugar
> ½ small cucumber, diced
> 1 quart sparkling water

Blend all but sparkling water until cucumber is liquefied. Let stand in refrigerator several hours. Strain over block of ice and add charged water.

Rhubarb Punch

(8 to 10 servings)

Unusual, and very good.

Cook until tender, then chill

> 3 cups diced pink rhubarb
> 1 cup sugar
> 3 cups water

Blend ½ at a time until rhubarb is liquefied. Pour over ice in punch bowl and add

> 1 cup pineapple juice
> 1 pint ginger ale
> 3 tablespoons lemon juice

Tomato Sauerkraut Cocktail

(For 3)

Zesty and robust; a good appetizer.

> 1 cup tomato juice
> ½ cup packed sauerkraut, with juice
> 1 thin slice onion
> 3 or 4 sprigs parsley
> 1 cup cracked ice

Blend until vegetables are liquefied.

Vegetable Cocktail

(4 or 5 appetizer drinks)

A real tantalizer!

> 1 can (1 pint 2 oz.) tomato juice
> 1 small rib celery, with leaves, cut up
> 2 or 3 sprigs parsley
> 2 slices lemon, with peel
> 1 slice green pepper
> 1 slice onion
> ¼ teaspoon salt
> ½ teaspoon sugar
> 1 cup cracked ice

Blend until vegetables are completely liquefied.

COFFEE, CHOCOLATE AND TEA DRINKS

I am not going to tell you how to make coffee, chocolate and tea. You already know how. But maybe you don't know how many delicious beverages the blender will perfect, beginning with these staples. Some of them would be impossible to make without a blender.

COFFEE AND CHOCOLATE

Cinnamon Coffolate

(2 tall ones)

Coffee, chocolate and cinnamon are a harmonious threesome.

> 1 ounce unsweetened chocolate, melted
> 2 cups cold milk
> 1 tablespoon instant coffee
> 1½ tablespoons sugar (more if you like sweet drinks)
> Few grains salt
> ¼ teaspoon cinnamon
> 1 cup cracked ice

Blend about 30 seconds. Serve topped with whipped cream and a sprinkle of cinnamon.

Coffee Carrousel

(One 12-ouncer)

You could flavor this with real rum.

> 1 cup milk
> 1½ teaspoons instant coffee
> 1 tablespoon sugar
> ⅛ teaspoon rum extract
> 2 tablespoons (big ones) chocolate ice cream

Blend 30 seconds. If this is for a party, float more ice cream on top and stick a tiny opened paper parasol into the ice cream.

Coffee Peach Fluff

(1 tall drink)

Delectable!

½ cup cold water
1 teaspoon instant coffee
¼ cup lightly thawed quick-frozen peaches
1 tablespoon sugar
1 egg white
Few drops vanilla or almond extract

Blend 30 seconds. Put an ice cube into the glass. Best when *very* cold.

Frosted Coffee

(For 2)

Thick and creamy.

2 cups cold water
1½ tablespoons instant coffee
1 pint vanilla ice cream

Blend until thick and fluffy.

Hot Marshmallow Cocoa

(2 servings)

An old treat in a new form.

Cook 2 or 3 minutes, stirring

2 tablespoons sugar
2 tablespoons cocoa
½ cup water

Add and heat thoroughly

1½ cups milk
Dash salt

Pour into warm blender container and blend a minute with

4 marshmallows

Iced Mint Chocolate

(3 tall ones)

Very chocolatey, and absolutely no "canned" milk taste; rich and delicious!

Cut into small pieces, into the blender

2 1-ounce squares chocolate

Add

½ cup sugar
½ cup hot water

Blend a minute, then add

¼ teaspoon salt
1 can (13 ounces) evaporated milk
¼ teaspoon vanilla
¼ teaspoon peppermint flavoring, or 4 or 5 sprigs fresh mint
1 cup cracked ice

Keep hand on blender cover when you start the motor as this is a full load. Blend about a minute. Serve in tall glasses. Whipped cream or a small spoonful of ice cream may be used for garnish if you wish.

TEA DRINKS

Currant Tea Punch

(4 tall glasses)

Like pink tea?

1 cup currant jelly
1 cup cold water
2 teaspoons instant tea
¼ cup lemon juice
½ cup orange or pineapple juice
1 cup cracked ice

Blend 15 seconds, pour into glasses, fill with sparkling water and garnish with mint sprigs if you have them.

Frosted Tea

(For 2)

Better than it sounds.

1 cup cold water
2 teaspoons instant tea
½ pint lemon, lime, orange or pineapple sherbet

Blend just a few seconds, until thick and foamy, pour into glasses and fill with ginger ale. Garnish with mint or a cherry.

Iced Tea Hollywood

(For 2)

How to cool off in July.

2 cups cold water
1½ tablespoons instant tea
2 tablespoons lime or lemon juice
4 maraschino cherries
2 teaspoons sugar
1 cup cracked ice

Blend and pour into glasses with more ice. Put a couple of mint sprigs into the blender with this drink if you wish.

THE MILK BAR

Apricot Shake

(For 2)

Equally good with fresh or dried fruit.

> 1 cup canned apricots or ½ cup cooked dried apricots
> 1 cup milk
> Few drops almond extract
> ½ pint vanilla ice cream

Blend until thick and fluffy.

Orange Buttermilk

(For 2)

Even if you don't care much for buttermilk, you should like this refresher.

> ½ cup orange juice
> 2 tablespoons sugar
> Inch-square piece of outer rind of orange
> 1½ cups buttermilk

Blend about 20 seconds. Try this with yogurt, too—delicious!

Grape Buttermilk Punch

(2 drinks)

A little sweet, a little sharp.

> ¼ cup grape juice
> 2 tablespoons lemon juice
> 1 pint buttermilk
> 2 tablespoons sugar

Blend about 15 seconds.

Danish Buttermilk Drink

(For 2)

Just tart enough.

> 2 tablespoons sugar
> 1 egg
> 1 pint buttermilk
> 1 tablespoon lemon juice
> Square inch of pared outer rind of lemon

Run the blender for about 20 seconds.

Maple Egg Shake

(2 servings)

Sweet and lovely!

> 3 tablespoons maple sirup, or brown sugar
> Few grains salt
> 1 egg
> 2 cups milk
> ¼ teaspoon vanilla

Blend 15 to 20 seconds.

Maple Shake

(2 servings)

Delicious with a sandwich lunch.

> ¼ cup maple sirup
> ½ teaspoon vanilla
> 2 cups milk
> ½ pint vanilla ice cream

Cover and blend until foamy. If you want a very thick shake, use less milk and more ice cream.

Chocolate Malted Milk

(1 glass)

A teenager's joy.

> 1 cup cold milk
> 2 tablespoons malted milk
> 2 tablespoons canned chocolate sirup or 1½ table-
> spoons sweet cocoa mix
> 1 scoop ice cream

Blend until thick and fluffy. Add an egg for an egg malt and, perhaps, a few drops of vanilla.

Chocolate Shake with Banana

(For 2)

Let the young ones make it themselves.

> 2 cups milk
> 1 egg
> 1 banana, cut in pieces
> ¼ cup canned chocolate sirup
> Few grains salt

Blend about a minute. This is good with ½ coffee and ½ milk too.

Jam Shake

(For 1)

Youngsters love this after school.

> 2 tablespoons strawberry jam or apricot or cherry
> preserves
> 1 cup cold milk
> Dash nutmeg

Blend about 10 seconds.

Milk Fruit Shrub

(1 tall one)

An old-timer, modernized.

> ½ cup any fresh berries
> 1 to 3 tablespoons sugar
> 1 tablespoon lemon juice
> 3 tablespoons orange juice
> Few grains salt
> 1 cup cold milk

Blend 30 seconds to 1 minute.

Orange Milk

(2 glasses)

Good for the youngsters.

> 1 cup orange juice
> 1 cup milk
> 2 teaspoons sugar

Blend just a few seconds. An egg will turn this into orange eggnog, and then a sprinkle of nutmeg is appropriate. Or fancy it up by adding a scoop or two of orange sherbet.

Peach or Pear Shake

(For 1)

There's no season for canned fruit.

> 2 halves of canned pears or peaches
> ⅔ cup milk
> 2 tablespoons sirup from canned fruit
> 2 small scoops vanilla ice cream

Blend about 15 seconds.

Fresh Peach Shake

(For 2)

This one's double peachy!

> 1 cup diced fresh peaches
> ¼ cup sugar
> 2 tablespoons lemon juice
> 1 cup milk
> ½ pint peach or vanilla ice cream

Blend until thick and fluffy.

Peppermint Milk

(1 glass)

Pretty pink and minty; should be very cold.

> 1 cup cold milk
> 2 sticks peppermint candy, broken in pieces

Blend about 15 seconds. I made this with buttermilk by mistake once and have frequently made it that way on purpose, since. We use the Christmas tree's candy canes this way.

Pineapple Smoothie

(For 2)

The flavor is tropical.

> 1 cup fresh diced pineapple
> 2 tablespoons sugar
> 1 cup milk
> ½ cup cracked ice

Blend about 30 seconds to a minute.

Prune Milk

(1 tall drink)

Try this for breakfast.

¼ cup cooked pitted prunes, packed in cup
1 cup milk
Few drops vanilla or sprinkle of cinnamon
½ cup cracked ice

Blend until prunes are liquefied. This is good with an egg, too, or a scoop of ice cream.

Strawberry Milk

(For 2)

So pretty and so good!

1½ cups milk
½ package frozen strawberries or 1 pint fresh strawberries plus ¼ cup sugar

Blend about 30 seconds.

Strawberry Shake

Add 2 big scoops of vanilla ice cream to the preceding recipe.

Strawberry Malted

Add the ice cream plus ¼ cup plain malted milk.

SODAS MADE IN THE BLENDER

These are even better than orthodox sodas. You simply put the ice cream, flavoring and a little milk or fruit juice in the blender, blend just a few seconds, until thick, pour it into a soda glass and fill with sparkling water. The following recipe will serve as a pattern for any fruit soda.

Strawberry Soda

(For 1)

A pink delight!

⅓ cup frozen or crushed sweetened strawberries
1 large scoop vanilla or strawberry ice cream
3 tablespoons milk or sparkling water

Blend 20 seconds or until smooth and thick, pour into glass and fill with sparkling water.

7

Entrees

The blender's ability to combine ingredients and reduce them to coarse or fine particles for a sauce carries over to the preparation of many entrees. In a few cases, the blender is useful in actually mincing food to a paste, as demonstrated by the recipe for Halibut Mousse. Curries and spaghetti sauces are so much quicker and easier if you let the blender help.

This collection of recipes will show you the way to easier preparation of many main dishes and perhaps will encourage you to undertake a few recipes that otherwise might seem like too much work.

Codfish Delight

(6 servings)

Cod in a cheese custard.

Run cold water for 15 minutes over

> 2 cups salt codfish

Cover with cold water and heat slowly to the boiling point, drain and repeat 2 or 3 times to soften fish and remove excess salt. Shred. Meanwhile, in blender container place

> 2⅔ cups milk
> 2 tablespoons butter

194

1 slice onion
2 eggs
1 slice green pepper
½ cup diced cheese

Blend about 20 seconds and combine with fish in buttered casserole. Mix in

1 cup blender-made crumbs (2 slices bread)

Top with

½ cup blender-made crumbs (1 slice bread)
2 tablespoons melted butter

Bake in pan of hot water at 350° for 40 minutes.

Codfish in Spanish Sauce

(3 or 4 servings)

Such good flavor!
Blender-chop

2 onions, quartered

Sauté in

¼ cup olive oil with
2 pimientos, diced

In blender container place

½ cup white wine
½ cup parsley
½ teaspoon salt

Blend until parsley is chopped fine. Add to sautéed onions with

1 family-size can (15 ounces) tomato sauce

Simmer gently 30 minutes. Add

1 pound fresh or frozen (thawed) codfish

Spoon sauce over fish and simmer another 20 minutes or until fish flakes easily. If sauce thickens too much, add a little water.

Fish Fillets, Portuguese Style

(6 servings)

Garlicky, it's true, but deliciously sauced.

In blender container place

> 3 cloves garlic
> 5 or 6 sprigs parsley
> 1 teaspoon salt
> ½ teaspoon cumin seed
> ⅓ cup catsup
> ¼ cup wine vinegar
> ½ green pepper, cut in pieces
> 1 small onion, quartered

Blend until vegetables are finely chopped. Pour into saucepan and add

> 1½ cups water or fish or chicken stock, or water and white wine

Simmer sauce for 30 minutes. Meanwhile place in buttered shallow baking pan

> 2 pounds fish fillets

Pour sauce over fillets and bake at 400° for 25 minutes.

Or cook down sauce until fairly thick and serve it over the fillets which you have dipped in egg and crumbs and fried until brown. This is the Portuguese way, but the other is simpler.

Mushroom-Stuffed Fish Turbans

(6 servings)

Coiled fillets baked in muffin pans are attractive, and good.

Sprinkle with lemon juice, salt and pepper, and coil in buttered muffin pans

> 2 pounds thawed cod, haddock, ocean perch or other fillets

Crumb in blender and empty into bowl

> 4 slices soft bread, torn apart

Place in blender container

> ½ cup cream
> 2 eggs
> 3 or 4 sprigs parsley
> ½ cup fresh or canned mushrooms
> 1 slice onion
> ½ teaspoon salt
> ¼ teaspoon pepper

Blend until smooth, and add to bread crumbs. Cook gently over low heat until mixture thickens. Spoon it into centers of fish turbans. Bake at 400° for 15 to 20 minutes, or until fish flakes easily. If you think you need a sauce, make it tomato or mushroom.

Halibut Mousse

(8 servings)

This is an elegant entree for a very special luncheon.

Remove skin and bones from

> 3-pound halibut steak

Simmer skin and bones for ½ hour with

> 1 teaspoon salt
> 4 peppercorns
> 1 bay leaf
> 2 cups water

Meanwhile, take a sharp knife to the raw fish and cut it into large dice. Measure

> 1 cup cream

Place ⅓ of the cream and ⅓ of the fish in the blender container at a time, and mix to a thick paste. This will require stopping the motor frequently to work the mixture down with your rubber spatula. It is best to start with just 2 or 3 cubes of fish, adding the others gradually. To the last batch of cream and fish add

> 1½ teaspoons salt
> ¼ teaspoon white pepper

Turn minced fish into bowl and add

> 4 slices bread, crumbed in blender
> ¼ cup white table wine

Mix well and fold in

> 6 egg whites, beaten stiff

Turn into a well-buttered fish mold or loaf pan, cover with aluminum foil and place mold or pan in a pan of hot water. Bake at 325° for 1½ hours. Let mousse stand 10 minutes, then unmold on a deep platter and pour the following sauce over it.

Sauce for Halibut Mousse

Place in blender container

> 1 cup fish stock (from cooking bones and skin)
> ¼ cup soft butter
> ¼ cup flour
> ¼ cup packed parsley
> ½ teaspoon salt
> ¼ teaspoon pepper
> 1 egg

Blend smooth and turn into saucepan with

> 1 cup cream

Cook and stir over low heat until smooth and thick, then add

> ¼ cup white wine

Stir and cook a minute or so longer, but do not allow sauce to boil. Taste for seasoning and add more salt if you need it.

Deviled Salmon in Sea Shells

(6 servings)

Lemon is the secret.

Place in blender container

> 1 cup canned tomato soup, undiluted
> ¼ onion
> ¼ green pepper, diced
> 3 tablespoons butter
> ½ teaspoon salt
> 1 teaspoon prepared mustard
> 1 slice lemon, including peel

Blend about 15 seconds and pour over

> 1 pound canned salmon, flaked

Pile in baking shells or ramekins and top with, in order,

> ½ cup crumbs (1 slice bread, blender-crumbed)
> 3 tablespoons melted butter
> 6 thin slices lemon (1 per serving)
> Paprika

Bake at 400° about 25 minutes.

Sea Scallop

(8 servings)

A combination of salmon and tuna, company-seasoned.

Blender-chop

1 small onion
1 rib celery with tops, cut in 1-inch pieces

Add, in saucepan, to

¼ cup butter

Sauté for 5 minutes and add

2 teaspoons curry powder
½ teaspoon salt
¼ cup flour

Stirring constantly, add gradually

2 cups milk

Cook until thickened and smooth. Add to sauce

1 pound can red salmon, flaked
1 7-ounce can tuna, flaked

Turn mixture into scallop shells or shallow baking dish.
Sprinkle with

½ cup blender-chopped nuts

Bake at 350° for 25 minutes.

Tuna with Brazil Nuts

(4 servings)

A quickie for lunch.

Cut fine in blender, a few at a time, emptying the container
into a bowl

1 cup Brazil nuts

Place in blender container

¼ cup butter
2 cups milk
¼ cup flour
¾ teaspoon salt
⅛ teaspoon pepper

2 pimientos
½ teaspoon worcestershire sauce

Blend until pimientos are coarsely cut—just a second or two —turn into saucepan and cook until thickened. Add, breaking apart

> 1 7-ounce can tuna

Add nuts previously prepared. Bake in small greased baking dish for 15 minutes at 350°.

Tuna Loaf

(6 to 8 servings)

A good choice for the Ladies' Aid luncheon.

Crumb in blender

> 8 slices bread, torn apart (1 slice at a time, emptying container between times)

Place in container

> 1 can condensed mushroom soup
> 1 cup milk
> ½ teaspoon salt
> ¼ teaspoon paprika
> 2 eggs
> 1 pimiento

Blend smooth and pour over crumbs and

> 2 7-ounce cans tuna, flaked

Bake in greased 1½-quart loaf pan at 350° for 45 minutes. Serve with White Sauce (page 275) or mushroom sauce made with another can of the soup.

Deviled Clams

(6 servings)

A popular way to serve clams out of the shell.

Crumb fine in blender and set aside

> 1 slice buttered bread, torn in pieces

Blender-chop

> 1 small onion, quartered
> 1 rib celery, cut in pieces

Sauté in

> ¼ cup butter with
> 1 clove garlic

Remove garlic and add

> 1 tablespoon flour
> ¾ teaspoon salt
> ¼ teaspoon each: pepper, thyme
> 3 drops tabasco sauce
> 1 tablespoon chili sauce

Drain and blender-chop

> 1 pint shucked clams

Add clams to seasoned mixture and cook until thickened, stirring constantly. Turn off heat and stir in

> ½ cup cracker meal
> 1 beaten egg
> 2 tablespoons clipped parsley

Place in six buttered shells, sprinkle with prepared crumbs and bake at 400° for 10 minutes.

Baked Crabmeat

(6 servings)

Beautifully seasoned!

In blender container place

> 1 cup chicken broth or cream
> 1 slice onion
> ¼ green pepper, cut in pieces

Sliver of garlic
¼ cup flour
¼ teaspoon curry powder
1 teaspoon paprika
½ teaspoon salt
Fleck cayenne pepper

Blend until vegetables are fine, pour into saucepan and cook and stir until thickened and smooth, adding

1 tablespoon butter
½ cup sour cream
1 can (6 or 7 ounces) crabmeat, flaked

Place mixture in six individual baking dishes and sprinkle with

½ cup grated sharp cheese

Bake until hot, about 10 minutes, at 400°.

Baked Seafood Salad

(6 servings)

Deserves its popularity.

Place in blender container

¾ cup mayonnaise
1 tablespoon worcestershire sauce
1 tablespoon lemon juice
½ large green pepper, in pieces
2 large ribs celery, sliced
1 slice onion
½ teaspoon salt
Dash pepper

Blend until vegetables are chopped fairly fine. Add

1 cup cooked or canned shrimp
1 can (6-7 ounces) crabmeat, flaked coarsely

Turn into individual greased shells. Place in blender

6 soda crackers, broken
½ cup cheese, diced

Blend until crackers and cheese form fine crumbs. Top casseroles. Bake 30 minutes in moderate oven, 350°. The mayonnaise in this combination gives it the salad name, and also makes a smooth, flavorsome binder for the fish.

Baked Stuffed Lobster Tails

(4 servings)

They're easy to eat this way!

Simmer for 9 minutes in water with 2 tablespoons salt, ½ teaspoon pepper and 2 tablespoons vinegar

4 lobster tails, 8 ounces each

In blender container place

¼ cup sherry or white table wine
¼ teaspoon paprika
Dash cayenne
4 parsley sprigs
1 slice onion
1 sliver garlic
½ teaspoon salt
¼ cup soft butter

Blend until mixture is chopped fine. Mix with

1 slice toast, broken apart and crumbed in blender

Cool lobster tails, cut away membrane and remove meat in one piece. Cut meat into bite-size pieces, fit back into shells and sprinkle with crumb mixture. Bake about 20 minutes at 350°.

Oyster Soufflé

(4 servings)

Easy, and very good.

Prepare

> 1 cup Thick White Sauce, page 276, using oyster
> liquor as part of liquid

Place in blender container

> 3 egg yolks
> 1 cup drained oysters
> ¼ teaspoon each: salt, paprika
> 1 slice onion
> ½ pimiento

Blend until oysters and vegetables are chopped fine. Mix with white sauce. Fold in

> 3 egg whites, beaten stiff

Bake in greased casserole set in a pan of hot water at 350° for 30 minutes or until firm in center. Serve at once.

East India Curry

(6 servings)

The curry sauce is equally good with turkey, lamb, veal and other meats.

In blender container place

> 1 cup chicken broth
> 1 large peeled tomato, quartered
> 2 medium onions, quartered
> 1 clove garlic
> 2 tablespoons curry powder
> 1 tablespoon paprika
> 1 teaspoon salt
> 2 tablespoons lemon juice

Blend until vegetables are chopped fine. Place in saucepan with

> 1 stick cinnamon
> 1 bay leaf
> 3 cloves

    2 tablespoons butter
    1 more cup broth

Simmer ingredients together for 15 minutes. Add

    2 pounds cooked, shelled shrimps

Cook 5 minutes longer. Thicken with mixture of

    2 tablespoons flour
    2 tablespoons water

Remove spices. Add

    ½ cup sour cream

Stir and serve over hot rice, accompanied by chutney and grated coconut, page 358, or canned flake coconut.

Hawaiian Curried Shrimps

(4 to 5 servings)

For discriminating guests.

Place in blender container

    1 cup milk
    6 tablespoons flour
    ⅓ cup soft butter
    1 tablespoon curry powder
    1¼ teaspoons salt
    2 or 3 pieces candied ginger (good sized pieces)
    1 slice onion
    2 tablespoons lemon juice

Blend smooth, then place in saucepan with

    2 cups coconut milk (prepared as for Hawaiian Coconut Pudding, page 121, only with water)

Cook and stir over low heat until sauce thickens and is smooth. Add and heat through

    1½ pounds peeled, deveined shrimps

Serve over

3 cups hot cooked rice

Accompany with curry condiments, including chutney, blender-chopped cashews, watermelon pickles, crumbled crisp bacon.

Shrimps de Jonghe

(6 servings)

A classic, from an old Chicago restaurant, made easier by the use of the blender.

Blender-crumb until fine and set aside

1½ slices bread

In blender container place

1 stick softened butter (½ cup)
1 clove garlic
¾ teaspoon salt
4 or 5 sprigs parsley
½ cup sherry
Dash each, cayenne and paprika

Blend until smooth. Mix with the reserved crumbs.

In six individual baking dishes place layers of buttery crumbs with

2 pounds cooked shrimps

Crumbs should be on top. Bake at 375° for 20 to 25 minutes.

Kidney Bean Rabbit

(6 servings)

A good lunch or late supper.

Blender-chop

1 medium onion, quartered
1 green pepper, cut in pieces

Sauté for 5 minutes in

2 tablespoons butter

Add

2 tablespoons catsup
2 teaspoons worcestershire
½ teaspoon salt
¼ teaspoon pepper
Speck cayenne pepper
½ pound cubed sharp process cheese
1 can kidney beans, drained

Heat together over low heat until cheese melts and mixture is very hot. Serve on toast.

Macaroni and Cheese Mousse

(6 servings)

A variation of a standard American dish.

Cook about 12 minutes in boiling salted water and drain

8 ounces macaroni (elbow or broken lengths)

Crumb in blender and set aside

2 slices white bread, torn apart

Place in blender container

3 eggs
1½ cups milk
1 teaspoon salt
⅓ cup butter
¼ cup packed parsley
1 small onion, in quarters
2 pimientos
½ pound American cheese, diced

Blend about 30 seconds and mix with macaroni. Add crumbs. Place in greased shallow baking dish, 9 by 12 inches, and set in a pan of hot water. Bake in moderate oven at 350° for an hour or until the custard sets. Serve plain or with a tomato sauce.

Spaghetti Loaf with Shrimp Sauce

(8 servings)

Ready for the oven in no time.

Cook in boiling salted water until tender

> 1½ cups broken spaghetti

Place in blender container

> 1 cup milk
> ¼ cup butter
> 3 egg yolks
> 1 cup diced cheese
> 5 sprigs parsley
> 1 pimiento
> ½ small onion
> 1 teaspoon salt
> ½ teaspoon pepper

Blend thoroughly and add to spaghetti. Add

> 1 cup soft crumbs (2 slices bread)

Fold in

> 3 egg whites, beaten stiff

Turn into greased loaf pan and bake at 350° for 1 hour. Turn out on hot platter and serve with Shrimp Sauce.

Shrimp Sauce

> 3 tablespoons butter or margarine
> 3 tablespoons flour
> 1½ cups milk

1 teaspoon worcestershire sauce
½ teaspoon salt
¼ teaspoon pepper
1 cup cooked shrimp or 1 5-ounce can

Blend until shrimp is chopped. Heat in a saucepan until thickened.

Swiss Fondue

(6 servings)

Fondue is tricky by the standard method. The blender has made success sure and easy.

Dice

1 pound Swiss Emmenthaler cheese

Grate cheese in blender, a third at a time, with

1½ cups white table wine (½ cup with each portion of cheese)
1 sliver garlic
2 tablespoons cornstarch
Sprinkle of nutmeg
Black pepper

Heat gently in fondue dish or chafing dish, stirring occasionally until mixture thickens and begins to bubble. Add

2 tablespoons kirsch

Use long-handled forks to spear chunks of crusty French bread and dip them into the fondue.

For the young, if you don't wish to use wine, substitute chicken stock, and omit the kirsch.

Puffy Omelet with Cheese

(6 servings)

Perfect for brunch.

Place in blender container

> ⅓ cup milk or water
> 1 cup diced cheddar or Swiss cheese
> 1 teaspoon salt
> ¼ teaspoon pepper
> 6 egg yolks
> Sprig or two of parsley

Blend just a few seconds to combine ingredients well. Fold into

> 6 egg whites, beaten stiff

Turn into well-greased skillet or omelet pan, spread evenly and cook slowly over low heat until puffed and delicately browned underneath. Then place in moderately hot oven, 375°, to brown top. Turn out onto heated serving plate and serve with White Sauce (page 275), a creamed vegetable or creamed fish. You needn't separate white and yolks of eggs for an omelet, but you get a puffier one if you do. Of course you can crease it down the center and serve it with the filling in the middle, a standard practice in serving omelets.

Beef and Noodle Mélange

(8 servings)

Your dinner, all in one pot.

Place in blender

> ¼ cup liquid from stuffed olives
> ½ cup stuffed olives
> 1 clove garlic
> 1 green pepper, diced
> 1 onion, quartered

Blend until finely chopped. In a skillet brown

> 1 pound ground beef in 2 tablespoons oil

Add blended sauce and

½ pound cheese, diced
¼ pound noodles, cooked
2 cups whole-kernel corn (canned, frozen or fresh)
2 cups tomatoes (canned or fresh)
Salt, pepper as needed

Turn into greased casserole. Cover and bake 45 minutes at 350°.

Beef Stroganoff

(6 servings)

One of a hundred variations of this popular dish, and one of the best of them.

Cut into strips about 2 inches long and ½ inch wide

1½ pounds round steak, ½ inch thick

Roll in mixture of

¼ cup flour
1½ teaspoons salt
½ teaspoon pepper

Brown strips well in

¼ cup oil

Meanwhile, in blender container place

1 cup beef broth or bouillon
1 medium onion, quartered
1 clove garlic
4 or 5 sprigs parsley
Leaves from one rib celery
1 dill pickle, in chunks

Blend until ingredients are chopped fine. Add to beef and cover pan. Cook gently until meat is very tender, about 1 hour. Sauté for a minute

½ pound sliced mushrooms, in
2 tablespoons butter

Add to meat with

> 1 cup sour cream

Heat through but do not boil. Serve hot.

Stuffed Flank Steak

(4 or 5 servings)

Easy, economical, and savory.

Have meat dealer score for you

> 1 flank steak, about 1½ pounds

Crumb in blender, not too fine, and empty into bowl

> 5 slices bread, torn apart

In blender container place

> ¼ cup beef bouillon or red wine
> 2 slices onion
> ¼ green pepper, cut in pieces
> 1 clove garlic, optional
> 2 ribs celery with leaves, cut in 1-inch pieces
> 1 teaspoon salt
> Pinch of salad herbs
> ¼ teaspoon pepper

Blend until vegetables are chopped. Drop in

> 1 egg

Blend a few seconds more and add to crumbs. Mix well, spread on steak and roll up lengthwise. Tie with string and brown all around in

> ¼ cup oil or drippings

Place in baking dish or dutch oven and lay over top of roll

> Strips of bacon, salt pork or fat ham

Add to pan

> 1 cup more bouillon

Cover and cook over low heat or in 325° oven 1½ to 2 hours.

Swiss Steak

(6 servings)

Long, slow cooking is the secret of tenderness.

Combine

> 1½ teaspoons salt
> ½ teaspoon pepper
> ¼ cup flour

Pound this mixture with meat tenderer or edge of saucer into both sides of

> 2 pounds round or rump steak, 1½ inches thick

Brown steak on both sides in

> 2 tablespoons oil or drippings

In blender container place

> 1 can (1 pound) tomatoes
> 1 clove garlic
> 2 medium onions, quartered
> 1 rib celery, sliced in 1-inch pieces
> 6 sprigs parsley

Blend until vegetables are chopped. Pour over steak. Add, if you wish

> A pinch of oregano or basil, or a bay leaf

Cover and cook gently on top of range or in 325° oven for 2 hours or until meat is very tender. If sauce thickens too much, thin it with

> Bouillon, water or red wine

Chili Pot Roast

(4 or more servings)

A flavorful way of fixing a less expensive cut of beef.

Place in blender

> 1 cup water
> 1 clove garlic
> ¼ cup packed parsley
> ¼ cup chili sauce
> ½ teaspoon worcestershire sauce

Blend 30 seconds. Brown on all sides

> 3 pounds beef chuck in
> 3 tablespoons drippings

Season with

> 2½ teaspoons salt
> ¼ teaspoon pepper

Add ¼ cup of the blended sauce, cover and cook over low heat or in 325° oven about 3 hours, adding remaining sauce from time to time. Remove meat to hot platter and thicken sauce for gravy. This can be done by blender-mixing flour and water as thickening (2 tablespoons flour per cup of total liquid).

Rump Pot Roast in Red Wine

(Serves a crowd—12 or more)

This is my favorite dish for an informal gathering.

Brown on all sides in heavy pan

> 6 pounds rolled rump roast

Season with salt, pepper, a sprinkle of dried mixed herbs. In blender container place

> 1 cup red wine (dry)
> 1 or 2 cloves garlic
> 2 onions, quartered
> 1 green pepper, diced
> 2 skinned fresh tomatoes

Blend until vegetables are chopped. Add to browned roast with

> 1 slice lemon
> 1 branch celery with leaves
> 1 bay leaf

Cover and cook gently until very tender, 3 or 4 hours. Gravy may be thickened with flour and extended with bouillon or more wine. Remove strings. Slice meat thin and serve it in the gravy.

Good, Good Meat Balls

(6 servings)

Good on spaghetti, noodles or rice.

Crumb in blender and empty into bowl

> 1 slice toast, broken apart

Blender-chop and add to crumbs

> 2 ribs celery, cut in 1-inch pieces
> 1 green pepper, cut in squares
> 1 medium onion, quartered

Place in blender container

> 1 egg
> 4 or 5 sprigs parsley
> 1 clove garlic
> 1 teaspoon worcestershire sauce
> 1½ teaspoons salt
> ½ teaspoon pepper
> Pinch of thyme

Blend fine and add to bowl with

> 1 pound ground chuck beef
> ½ pound ground veal

Mix well and shape into balls about 1 inch in diameter. Brown all around in

> ¼ cup butter or oil

Add

> 1 can (1 pint, 2 ounces) tomato juice

Cover and simmer gently or bake at 325° for 45 minutes.

Monterey Pancakes

(4 servings)

With salad, you have a good meal.

> 1 cup milk
> 1 egg
> 1 tablespoon salad oil
> ½ cup whole-kernel corn, drained
> 1 cup pancake mix

Blend a few seconds and bake 8 pancakes on a hot, lightly greased griddle, turning once. Stack, cover and keep warm.

In blender container place

> 1 can (8 ounces) tomato sauce
> 1 can (6 ounces) tomato paste
> 1 green pepper, cut in pieces
> 1 onion, quartered

Blend until vegetables are chopped. Brown in a little butter or drippings

> 1 pound ground beef, seasoned with
> 1 teaspoon salt
> ¼ teaspoon pepper

Add the tomato sauce. Simmer 10 minutes and serve meat mixture between and over corn pancakes, two to a customer.

Cheese Meat Loaf

(8 or more servings)

A good one to freeze ahead, if you wish.

Blender-crumb and chop together, then transfer to bowl

> 5 slices toast, broken apart
> 1 cup diced sharp cheese

Place in blender container

> 2½ cups tomato purée or sauce
> 3 eggs
> ¼ teaspoon thyme
> 1 small bay leaf
> 1 tablespoon salt
> ½ green pepper, cut in pieces
> 1 large onion, cut in eighths
> Sprinkle of garlic salt

Blend until vegetables are cut fine. Mix with crumbs, cheese and

> 2½ pounds ground beef

Bake in oiled loaf pan at 350° for 1 hour if you wish to freeze the loaf, 1½ hours if not. Cool and chill the loaf quickly for freezing. Wrap in freezing materials and freeze. To reheat, cover loaf with tomato sauce or gravy and place in 400° oven for an hour. Loaf is good cold as well as hot.

Meat Loaf Delicious

(8 or more servings)

Perfectly seasoned.

Place in blender container

> 1 egg
> ½ cup water

> 1 small onion, quartered
> Tops from 4 or 5 ribs celery, in pieces
> 4 or 5 sprigs parsley
> 2 teaspoons salt
> ½ teaspoon sage
> ¼ teaspoon pepper

Blend until vegetables are chopped. Mix with

> 2 pounds ground beef
> ½ pound bulk pork sausage

Pack into loaf pan and bake at 350° for 1 hour and 15 minutes. This loaf is good hot or cold, and it can be sliced into neat, thin slices when cold, so the leftovers are fine for Sunday night.

Austrian Veal Goulash

(4 servings)

An unusual combination to serve with boiled noodles, if you wish.

Blender-chop

> 3 large onions, cut in eighths

Sauté onions 5 minutes until soft and golden in

> ¼ cup butter

Add

> 1½ pounds veal, cut into 1-inch cubes
> 1 tablespoon paprika
> 1 teaspoon salt
> A little pepper

Cook and stir for 5 minutes.

Blender-chop in 1½ cups stock or bouillon

> 1 green pepper, cut in pieces
> 2 peeled fresh tomatoes (or 2 canned ones)

Add to meat mixture, cover and simmer for 1 hour. Stir in

> 2 tablespoons capers with liquid
> 1 cup sour cream

Heat through but do not boil.

Veal and Macaroni Casserole

(6 servings)

A prize-winning combination you'll make again and again.

Blender-chop separately

> 1 medium onion, quartered
> 1 green pepper, in pieces

Sauté in a little oil for 2 to 5 minutes, remove from pan and add to pan

> 2 pounds veal steak, ½ inch thick, cut in 1-inch cubes

Brown veal on all sides. Add the chopped onion and green pepper, also

> 1½ teaspoons salt
> ¼ teaspoon pepper
> 1 cup water

Cover and cook slowly until meat is tender. Thicken with paste made by mixing

> 2 tablespoons flour
> ¼ cup water

Stir constantly while cooking. Add, and heat through

> 1 package (7 or 8 ounces) macaroni, cooked
> 1 package frozen peas and carrots, cooked
> 2 cups sour cream

Do not boil after adding cream. Serve hot with crusty bread and salad.

Spicy Roast of Veal

(8 servings)

Piquantly seasoned and cooked gently for a long time.

Rub with oil

> 5-pound veal rump roast

Coat with mixture of

> 3 tablespoons flour
> 1 tablespoon dry mustard
> 1½ teaspoons salt
> ½ teaspoon pepper
> ½ teaspoon marjoram

Brown meat well in ¼ cup more oil.

In blender container place

> ½ cup bouillon
> ½ cup red wine vinegar
> 2 medium onions, quartered
> 6 or 8 sprigs parsley
> 2 teaspoons celery seeds

Blend until onions are chopped and pour over veal. Cover and cook gently on top of the range or in oven at 325° for 2 hours. Add to pan

> 16 small whole potatoes, pared
> 16 small whole carrots, scraped

Add salt and pepper for the vegetables, cover and cook 30 minutes, then add

> 1 pound green beans

Season beans and continue cooking 1 hour or until all vegetables are tender. Add stock from time to time if needed.

Veal Birds en Casserole

(6 servings)

A one-dish meal nice enough for a party.

Prepare in blender and set aside

> 2 cups soft bread crumbs
> ¼ cup finely chopped parsley

Chop in blender

> 2 medium onions, quartered

Sauté onion for 5 minutes in

> ¼ cup butter

Add to reserved crumbs, parsley, also

> 1 teaspoon salt
> ¼ teaspoon pepper
> 2 tablespoons cream

Place this filling on

> 6 slices veal steak, pounded flat (1½ pounds, cut
>   ¼ inch thick, cut in portions and flattened)

Cover filling with

> 6 slices boiled ham

Roll up each portion and tie with string. Brown all around in

> ¼ cup butter

Add

> 1 cup chicken broth
> 1 cup sliced carrots

Cover and cook gently 1 hour or until tender. Remove meat to warm platter. To drippings and carrots in pan add

1 cup chicken broth
2 tablespoons flour mixed smooth in blender with
½ cup more chicken broth

Cook and stir until gravy is thickened. Adjust seasonings as necessary and serve with veal birds (remove strings before serving).

Wonderful Lamb Stew

(Four to six servings)

It's all tenderness and flavor!

Brown in a little butter or oil

> 2 to 3 pounds boneless lamb cut for stew, well floured

Sprinkle with

> 2 teaspoons salt
> ½ teaspoon pepper
> Pinch of thyme
> Pinch of sugar

In blender container place

> 1 cup water or lamb stock (from boiling bones)
> 1 medium onion, quartered
> 1 rib celery, diced
> 1 carrot, sliced
> 1 clove garlic
> 2 fresh peeled or canned tomatoes

Blend until vegetables are chopped fine. Pour over browned lamb, adding

> 1 cup more water or stock
> ¾ cup red, white or pink table wine

Cover and cook gently for 1½ hours. Add

>   4 to 6 small whole potatoes
>   4 to 6 small whole carrots
>   4 to 6 small whole onions or turnips

Season well with

>   Salt, pepper

Cover and simmer until vegetables are tender.

Lamb Watercress Roll

(Six servings)

The unusual stuffing imparts a delightful flavor.

In blender container place

>   1 cup water
>   1 medium onion, quartered
>   1 bunch watercress

Blend until chopped fine. Drain liquid and save it. Mix with cress and onion

>   1 teaspoon salt
>   ½ teaspoon celery salt
>   ½ teaspoon paprika
>   Dash cayenne pepper

Spread mixture over cut side of

>   Boned shoulder of lamb

Roll up and tie meat firmly. Place in kettle with drained liquid, and

>   ½ cup white wine vinegar
>   3 cups water or chicken stock

Cover and simmer 2 hours. Remove meat from stock, wipe dry, spread with

>   Soft butter

Sprinkle with

Salt, pepper
½ cup fine blender-made crumbs

Bake in shallow roaster at 350° for about 45 minutes. Remove strings. Serve with gravy made from stock.

Ham Omelet

(For 2)

This is the basic method for the plain omelet.

In blender container place

3 eggs
½ cup diced cooked ham (or chicken or cheese)
3 tablespoons milk or cream

Cover and blend a few seconds. Pour out into hot skillet in which you've melted

2 tablespoons butter

Sprinkle with

Salt and pepper

Cook over low heat, lifting edges of omelet with spatula to let uncooked part run underneath. When cooked through but still soft and damp on top, fold or roll and slide omelet onto a hot platter.

Ham Loaf with Raisins

(6 servings)

An unusual loaf with lots of flavor.

Blender-crumb, not too fine, and set aside

4 slices bread, torn apart

Place in blender container

1 cup milk
2 tablespoons brown sugar

> 1 slice onion
> ½ cup raisins
> 1 tablespoon each: horseradish, prepared mustard
> ½ teaspoon salt
> 1 can (4 ounces) pimiento

Blend to chop onion, raisins and pimiento. Add gradually and blend to chop, not too fine

> 3 cups diced ham

Add and blend a few seconds

> 3 eggs

Mix with crumbs and turn into greased loaf pan about 9 by 5 inches. Bake at 350° for an hour and 15 minutes.

Pineapple Stuffed Pork Chop Roast

(6 servings)

Pre-carved, handsome, and easy to serve!

Brown on both sides in a little butter or oil, season with salt and pepper, and set aside

> 6 pork chops, about ¾ inch thick

Toast lightly in the oven

> 4 cups blender-prepared coarse bread crumbs

Chop in blender

> 1 medium onion, quartered
> ½ green pepper, in pieces
> 2 ribs celery, in inch pieces

Sauté these vegetables for 5 minutes in

> 2 tablespoons butter

Combine with crumbs, add and mix lightly

> 1 can (13½ ounces) pineapple tidbits, drained (save juice)
> 1 teaspoon salt

1 teaspoon mixed salad herbs
¼ teaspoon pepper

Stand the pork chops in a loaf pan, fat side up, and place the bread stuffing between them. Hold chops together with metal skewers. Pour pineapple juice over "roast" and bake 1½ hours at 325°.

Barbecued Chicken

(4 servings)

There'll be no complaints!

Place in paper bag

>   ¼ cup flour
>   2 teaspoons salt
>   ¼ teaspoon pepper

Shake in the bag with the flour mixture, a few pieces at a time

>   1 frying chicken, cut up

Brown all around in

>   ½ cup hot butter

In blender container place

>   1 cup water
>   1 cup catsup
>   1 onion, quartered
>   1 rib celery and top, sliced
>   ¼ green pepper, cut in pieces
>   2 tablespoons worcestershire sauce
>   2 tablespoons brown sugar

Blend until vegetables are chopped. Pour over chicken in skillet or casserole, cover and bake at 350° for 1 hour.

Add

>   1 package (10 ounces) frozen corn, cooked according to directions

Broiled Chicken with Mushroom Sauce

(4 or 8 servings)

The sauce makes the dish.

Brush well with butter and broil about 20 minutes on each side

> 2 young broiler chickens, split or quartered

Season with salt and pepper. Place in blender

> 2 cups chicken stock or bouillon
> ½ medium-sized onion, cut in pieces
> ¼ cup flour
> 1 teaspoon salt (less if stock is salty)
> ⅛ teaspoon pepper
> 1 teaspoon lemon juice
> 1 slice outer rind of lemon

Blend until onion is chopped fine. Sauté 5 minutes

> ½ pound fresh mushrooms, washed and dried, in
> ¼ cup butter or margarine

Add to blender and switch on motor for just a few seconds to chop mushrooms rather coarsely. Turn mixture into top of double boiler and cook over direct heat until thickened, stirring constantly. Add

> 2 tablespoons sherry

Keep hot over hot water. Serve with chicken.

Baked Turkey Hash

(6 servings)

A good pattern for any kind of hash.

Blender-chop

> 2 medium onions, quartered
> ½ green pepper, cut in pieces

Sauté for 5 minutes in

>2 tablespoons butter

Blender-chop in

>¾ cup turkey or chicken broth
>3 medium-size potatoes, diced

Blender-chop separately, not too fine

>3 cups diced turkey

Combine sautéed vegetables, potatoes and stock, turkey, and add

>2 teaspoons salt
>½ teaspoon pepper

Bake in buttered casserole 30 minutes at 350°, covered. Uncover and bake 30 minutes more. Mixture also may be baked in well-buttered skillet on top of range.

Turkey Cashew

(4 to 6 servings)

A post-Thanksgiving treat.

Crumb in blender

>1 slice white bread, broken

Turn into a small bowl or cup. Place in blender and chop coarsely

>¾ cup cashews

Turn into a second cup or place on waxed paper. Place in blender container

>1 cup cream
>¼ teaspoon sage
>1½ teaspoons salt
>Dash of pepper

¼ cup packed parsley
2 tablespoons sherry

Blend until parsley is chopped. Scatter ½ the chopped nuts on the bottom of a greased casserole and cover with ½ of

2 cups diced or sliced turkey

Add the rest of the nuts and the remainder of the turkey and cover with blended cream and seasonings. Top with the crumbs and a few broken cashews. Bake at 350°, moderate oven, about 25 minutes until browned.

Turkey Soufflé

(4 or more servings)

A delicate dish!

Blender-crumb and set aside

1 slice buttered toast, broken in pieces

Prepare

1 cup well-seasoned Thick White Sauce, page 276

In blender container place

6 sprigs parsley
1 slice onion
3 egg yolks

Blend to chop onion and parsley. Add to white sauce. Chop in blender, ½ cup at a time

1½ cups diced cooked turkey

Add to white sauce and season as necessary with salt, pepper, and paprika. Fold in

3 egg whites, beaten until stiff

Turn into buttered 1-quart casserole, sprinkle with the reserved crumbs and bake at 350° for about 40 minutes, or until firm in center. Serve plain or with mushroom sauce.

Chestnut Stuffing

(About 5 cups, for a capon or small turkey)

This delicious gourmet's treat could be baked in a pan as an accompaniment to poultry or meat, but is an unusual stuffing.

Simmer until tender*, then shell, skin and blender-chop

> 2 pounds chestnuts

Add

> 1 cup blender-made bread crumbs
> 1 teaspoon salt
> ⅛ teaspoon pepper
> ¼ cup melted butter
> ½ cup heavy cream

Mix lightly and fill the bird.

*Pare a little of the shell from one side of each with a sharp knife to make the shelling easier when chestnuts are cooked.

Pecan Crumble Stuffing

(For 10- to 12-pound turkey)

Crumb by hand, into a bowl

> 8 lightly toasted hamburger buns

Chop in blender and add

> 1 cup pecans

Chop in small amounts and add

> 2 large onions, cut in eighths
> 2 ribs celery with tops

Add also

> 2 teaspoons celery seed
> 2 teaspoons salt

1 tablespoon poultry seasoning
½ teaspoon pepper
3 sticks butter (1½ cups) melted

Toss ingredients together.

Brazil Nut Stuffing

(For a 10-pound turkey)

A different kind of dressing.

Crumb, a broken slice at a time, and empty blender container into bowl

15 slices white bread

Chop in ¼-cup lots and turn into bowl

2 cups whole Brazil nuts

Place in blender container

¼ cup water or stock
2 ribs celery with tops, sliced
2 small onions, quartered
1 tablespoon salt
1 teaspoon poultry seasoning
½ cup melted butter

Blend until vegetables are coarsely chopped. Mix with crumbs and nuts, and stuff bird. This is a light fluffy dressing with lots of flavor.

Croquettes

(4 servings)

Leftovers with a fresh-cooked taste.

Chop fine in blender, adding a few pieces at a time

1 cup diced cooked meat, chicken or fish

Turn into bowl with

½ cup blender-chopped cooked vegetables: green
beans, carrots—anything you may have in the
way of leftovers

Crumb fine in blender and add to meat and vegetables

1 slice bread, torn apart

Place in blender container

1 cup milk
½ teaspoon salt
¼ teaspoon pepper
¼ cup flour
1 slice onion
4 sprigs parsley

Blend a few seconds, turn into a saucepan and cook and stir
to a very thick sauce. Add to meat mixture, spread on a plate
and chill. Shape into 8 croquettes. Roll in

Fine dry crumbs (can be made in blender)

Dip in

1 egg, slightly beaten

Dip again into crumbs and fry in deep hot fat at 375° until
brown. Serve plain or with White Sauce (page 275), Jiffy
Cheese Sauce (page 281), mushroom or tomato sauce. Croquettes can be fried in shallow fat but aren't so evenly crisp-
coated and tempting.

Lamb or Chicken Curry

(6 servings)

This is real curry, but not too hot.

Place in blender container

1 cup meat stock or bouillon
1 onion, quartered and sautéed in
2 tablespoons butter

2 apples, sliced
3 tablespoons flour
2 tablespoons curry powder
¼ cup plum jam (or another kind)
¼ cup chutney
1 clove garlic

Blend until ingredients are chopped and add

½ cup raisins

Simmer for half an hour with

1 cup more stock

Serve over

3 cups diced cooked lamb or chicken

Accompany with fresh grated coconut (see page 358), more chutney, chopped cashews or peanuts.

Pork Chops with Cranberries

(6 servings)

A holiday season brightener.

Dredge with flour

6 inch-thick pork chops

Season with

1½ teaspoons salt
¼ teaspoon pepper

Brown in

3 tablespoons drippings

Place browned chops in casserole. Place in blender

¼ cup water
2 cups fresh cranberries
1 small orange, cut in pieces, peel included
½ cup sugar

Blend until fruit is fine. Pour over chops, cover casserole and bake in moderate oven at 350° for an hour or longer, until chops are very tender.

Baked Stuffed Spareribs

(6 servings)

Caraway subtly seasons the dressing.

Fry until crisp

>1 cup diced salt pork (½ pound)

Place in bowl and add

>1 cup diced tart apple
>1 cup sliced celery
>12 slices bread, crumbed

In blender container place

>¼ onion
>2 tablespoons sugar
>¼ cup packed parsley
>1 teaspoon salt
>¼ teaspoon pepper
>¼ cup water
>1 teaspoon caraway seeds

Blend about 20 seconds and add to other ingredients. Rub with salt and pepper

>4 small or 2 large sides of spareribs

Bake in 350° oven 45 minutes, then drain off fat, place dressing in pan and top with ribs. Bake 1 hour longer or until tender.

8 | Salads, Blender-Made

You can't *shred* cabbage for slaw in your blender but you can *chop* it and some of the best slaws are made this way. For many other chopped vegetables, the blender is wonderful. For example, you can blender-chop 2 or 3 carrots and sprinkle them over a bowl of mixed greens and tomatoes to give a pleasant crunchy effect.

When you want to sieve an avocado, grate a cucumber or mash a banana for a molded salad, the blender is your devoted slave. Presto! There's your mixture! The blender is also a speedy mixer of seasonings for an aspic or cream cheese as a base for a frozen fruit salad.

Salads should have texture and crispness; they shouldn't resemble baby food. So let's control the chopping action. Follow directions which come with your make of blender.

Molded Asparagus and Egg Salad

(6 servings)

Use fresh tips of asparagus if you can.

Place in blender container

> 1 tablespoon plain gelatin
> 1 cup hot water from asparagus

236

Blend a few seconds and add

> ½ teaspoon salt
> 1 slice onion
> 1 pimiento
> 1 tablespoon lemon juice
> ½ cup diced celery
> ¼ cup water or dry white wine

Blend until ingredients are chopped fine. Chill until mixture begins to thicken and add

> 3 hard-cooked eggs, diced
> 2 cups diced cooked asparagus
> 1 cup mayonnaise

Turn into large oiled mold; chill until firm and unmold on greens. Garnish with tomato quarters. Add a dab of mayonnaise (page 269) to each serving.

Party Avocado Mold

(10 to 12 servings)

Pleasingly tart; delectable!

Place in blender container

> 2 tablespoons plain gelatin
> ½ cup hot water

Blend a few seconds. Add

> 1½ cups orange juice
> 1 tablespoon sugar
> 1 teaspoon salt
> 2 tablespoons pickle relish
> ⅓ cup lemon juice
> Few drops tabasco sauce
> 1 thin slice onion
> 3 avocados, diced

Blend smooth and turn into large ring mold or individual molds and chill until firm. Turn out on greens and fill center of ring with orange and grapefruit sections. Accompany with mayonnaise. This is the perfect buffet-party salad.

Buffet Bean Salad

(8 servings or more)

This good mixture can grow—add green lima beans, too, if you like.

> ½ cup red wine vinegar
> ½ cup salad oil
> ½ cup sugar
> 1 teaspoon salt
> ½ teaspoon coarse black pepper
> 1 large onion, cut in chunks (sweet Spanish-type)
> 1 green pepper (seeds removed), cut in pieces

Blend until vegetables are chopped. Pour over contents of

> 1 can (1 pound) or 1 package cooked yellow wax beans, drained
> 1 can (1 pound) or 1 package cooked whole small green beans, drained
> 1 can (1 pound) kidney beans, drained and rinsed

Chill overnight before serving. This salad keeps well in the refrigerator.

Jellied Beet Salad

(6 servings)

Beautiful color in this salad; piquant flavor.

Place in blender container

> 1 package lemon gelatin
> 1 cup hot beet juice (from 1 pound can), and water

Blend a few seconds to dissolve gelatin. Add

> ¼ large lemon (no seeds)
> 1 teaspoon salt

½ small onion
1 tablespoon horseradish

Blend until ingredients are liquefied. Add

1 pound can beets, well drained

Blend until beets are chopped, not too fine. Turn into ring mold. Place in blender container

½ cup water
2 carrots, sliced
Tops of 2 celery ribs, cut in pieces

Blend until chopped. Add to beets in ring mold. Stir to mix. Chill until firm and serve with sour cream, or mayonnaise and sour cream combined. Curly endive, with its contrast of light and dark green, is a pretty garnish.

Carrot, Pickle and Peanut Salad

(4 servings)

Crunchy and appetizing.

Chop in blender in small amounts; empty into a bowl

6 medium carrots, cut in pieces
1 cup salted peanuts

Add and mix

2 tablespoons pickle relish
Mayonnaise to blend

Serve in lettuce cups.

Buffet Chicken Salad

(12 servings or more)

Pile it in a handsome bowl and garnish with greens.

Place in mixing bowl

>4 cups diced cooked chicken or turkey
>2 cups cooked elbow macaroni
>1 cup thin-sliced celery

In blender container place

>1 cup mayonnaise (page 269)
>¼ cup white table wine
>1 pimiento
>About 5 sprigs parsley
>½ green pepper, in pieces

Blend until vegetables are chopped. Add gradually and blend until chopped

>6 hard-cooked eggs, quartered
>1 cup toasted, salted pecans or almonds

Add this dressing to chicken, macaroni and celery, mix well and chill. Add salt, if necessary, and a little more mayonnaise if needed to moisten the salad.

Chicken Salad in Sherry Aspic

(Serves 10 at a buffet)

The wine makes it an aristocrat.

Place in blender top

>2 tablespoons plain gelatin
>½ cup hot chicken stock or chicken bouillon

Blend to dissolve. Add

>½ cup diced or sliced carrots
>1 thickish slice medium-sized onion
>½ cup diced celery
>About 3 sprigs parsley
>½ teaspoon salt
>¼ teaspoon pepper
>2 tablespoons lemon juice
>¼ cup sherry

Blend until vegetables are finely minced. Turn into large ring mold with

> 3 cups more chicken stock or bouillon
> 1½ cups diced cooked chicken
> ½ cup diced celery
> ½ cup cooked or canned peas

Chill until firm. Unmold on greens, and accompany with mayonnaise.

Rice and Chicken Salad

(4 servings)

If you've never had rice in a salad, you've missed something!

Mince in the blender on low speed or with quick on and off switches

> 1 rib celery, sliced
> 5 stuffed olives
> ½ green pepper, cut in pieces

Turn into a bowl with

> 2 cups cold cooked rice
> 1 small can boned chicken or turkey (1 cup)
> ½ cup mayonnaise (p. 269)
> 1 tablespoon chili sauce
> 1 tablespoon vinegar
> 1 tablespoon sugar
> 1 tablespoon cream
> 1 tablespoon pineapple juice (from canned pineapple slices)

Mix well. Chill in custard cups and turn each salad out onto a ring of pineapple placed on lettuce. Garnish with a dab of mayonnaise and a slice of stuffed olive for each. The rice stretches the good chicken flavor and gives a nice texture.

"The Best" Coleslaw

(6 servings)

A perfect accompaniment for fried fish or chicken.

Blender-chop separately with water; drain, then combine in a bowl

> ½ green pepper, in pieces
> 4 green onions with tops, in inch pieces
> 2 carrots, in slices (chop fine)
> Celery to make 1 cup, chopped
> Cabbage to make 6 cups, coarsely chopped

Add and mix lightly

> ½ cup thinly sliced radishes
> ½ cucumber, pared and diced
> 1½ teaspoons salt
> ¼ teaspoon pepper
> 3 tablespoons sugar
> ¾ cup salad oil
> ¾ cup white vinegar
> 4 or 5 ice cubes

Serve with the ice cubes in the salad.

Red and Green Slaw

(6 to 8 servings)

A pretty mixture with plenty of crunch.

Blender-chop separately in water, drain and combine in a bowl

> ½ medium green cabbage, cut in chunks
> ¼ medium red cabbage, cut in chunks
> 1 green pepper, in pieces
> 1 medium onion, quartered

Add mixture of

> ½ cup mayonnaise (page 269)
> 1 teaspoon salt
> 2 teaspoons sugar
> 1 tablespoon vinegar or lemon juice
> ¼ teaspoon pepper

Mix well and chill.

Sour Cream Slaw with Dill

(6 servings)

Garnish this one with green pepper rings.

Blender-chop, not too fine, in small amounts

> Crisp cabbage to make 4 cups
> Celery to make 1 cup
> ¼ cup packed parsley
> ½ medium onion

Place in bowl and add

> 1½ teaspoons dill seed
> 1 tablespoon lemon juice
> ½ cup sour cream
> ½ teaspoon (or more) salt
> Coarse black pepper

Toss lightly together with a fork. Serve chilled.

Crabmeat Salad

(8 servings)

Shrimps are good this way, too.

Place in blender top

> 2 tablespoons plain gelatin
> 1 cup hot water

Blend to dissolve and add

1 cup tomato sauce (8-ounce can)
½ pound cream cheese, softened
1½ cups diced celery
1 large green pepper, in pieces
1 slice onion

Blend until vegetables are chopped fine. Chill until slightly thickened and fold in

1 6½-ounce can crabmeat, flaked
1 cup mayonnaise (p. 269)

Turn into oiled mold and chill until firm. Unmold on greens and serve with mayonnaise.

Crab-Stuffed Tomato Salad

(4 servings)

A summertime luncheon favorite.

Blender-chop and empty into bowl

Celery to make 1 cup, chopped
Green pepper to make ½ cup
8 stuffed olives

Add and mix lightly with spoon

1 can (about 6½ ounces) crabmeat, flaked
½ cup mayonnaise (page 269), or Ever-So-Good Dressing (page 270)
1 tablespoon lemon juice
½ teaspoon salt
A little pepper

Spoon lightly into

4 peeled, hollowed tomatoes

Serve on lettuce. Avocado halves sprinkled with lemon juice are equally attractive receptacles.

Cranberry Jewel Salad

(6 servings)

A high-carat ruby.

Place in blender and switch on motor to dissolve

> 1 package raspberry gelatin
> 1¼ cups hot water

Cool somewhat and add

> 1 orange, cut in pieces (seeds removed, but not the peel)
> 1 pound can (about 1¾ cups) whole or jellied cranberry sauce, broken up

Blend until orange is finely chopped. Add

> ¼ cup port wine

Chill mixture in individual molds or 1 large one until firm. Serve on crisp lettuce.

Cranberry Relish Salad

(6 servings)

An easy way to make a classical favorite.

Place in blender container

> 1 package lemon-flavored gelatin
> 1 cup hot water

Blend a few seconds to dissolve gelatin and add

> 1 orange, quartered (seeds removed but not the peel)
> 1½ cups cranberries
> 1 apple, cored and sliced
> 1 cup sugar
> ¼ teaspoon salt

Blend until fruits are finely chopped. Add and blend for just a second

    ½ cup pecans

Turn into individual molds or into 1 large mold and chill until firm. Unmold on greens. Serve with a dressing made by combining mayonnaise and whipped cream in equal parts.

Delicious variation: Omit orange and add ½ pound cream cheese. Cut sugar to ⅔ cup.

Frozen Fruit Salad

(6 servings)

This one doubles as dessert.

Whip in blender and place in bowl

    1 cup heavy cream

In blender container place

    1 teaspoon plain gelatin
    3 tablespoons hot pineapple juice (from 9-ounce can crushed fruit)

Blend to dissolve gelatin. Add

    2 tablespoons lemon juice
    1 tablespoon maraschino cherry juice
    1 banana, in 3 pieces
    Dash of salt
    ⅓ cup mayonnaise (p. 269)

Blend smooth and add, with motor running

    12 marshmallows

When marshmallows are blended, fold mixture into whipped cream with

    1 9-ounce can crushed pineapple
    ½ cup quartered maraschino cherries

Freeze until firm in refrigerator tray. Cut into squares and serve on crisp greens.

Ham and Potato Salad Loaf

(6 servings)

Handsomest potato salad ever!

Line small loaf pan with wax paper (extend the wax paper up over the sides). Cover bottom and sides of pan with

> ½ pound thinly sliced baked ham

Place in blender container

> 1 tablespoon plain gelatin
> ¼ cup hot water

Blend to dissolve. Add

> 1 cup mayonnaise (page 269)
> 1½ teaspoons salt
> 1 slice onion
> 3 sprigs parsley
> 1 pimiento
> 2 ribs celery, cut

Blend until vegetables are chopped. Add mixture to

> 6 cups diced cooked potatoes
> 1 cup diced ham

Turn into loaf pan over ham slices and chill until firm. Turn out on platter and remove paper. Cut in thick slices to serve.

Killarney Salad

(6 servings)

But don't save it for St. Patrick's Day!

Place in blender container

> 1 package lime-flavored gelatin
> 1 cup hot water
> A few drops green food color

Blend until gelatin is dissolved. Add

> 1 tablespoon vinegar
> 3 medium carrots, scraped and sliced in chunks

Blend until carrots are grated fine. Add

> ½ cup salted peanuts

Blend until nuts are chopped. Add

> 1 can (1 pound 4½ ounces) crushed pineapple, not drained

Turn into 7-by-11-inch pan and chill until firm. Cut in squares and serve with mayonnaise on lettuce.

Mostaccioli Salad

(8 servings)

Use elbow or shell macaroni, if you'd rather. This is a good picnic or pot-luck dish.

In a bowl place

> 8 ounces mostaccioli (short cut), cooked
> 2 hard-cooked eggs, diced
> 1 cup sliced crisp celery or cauliflower

Grate in blender and add

> 3 large carrots, cut in inch pieces

In blender container place

> ¼ cup liquid from sweet pickles
> ¼ cup sliced sweet pickles
> ½ cup mayonnaise
> ½ green pepper, in pieces
> 1 teaspoon salt
> 2 green onions, with tops, in inch pieces

Blend until vegetables are chopped. Add to bowl with

> ½ pound sharp cheddar cheese, diced fine

Chill and serve on greens. Add more mayonnaise if necessary to moisten well.

Jellied Pineapple and Cucumber Salad with White Wine

(6 servings)

Has an Epicurean flavor.

Place in blender container

> 2 tablespoons plain gelatin
> 1 cup hot water

Blend to dissolve. Add

> 1 cup dry white wine
> 1 cucumber, in pieces
> 1 green pepper, in pieces
> 1 teaspoon salt
> ½ cup sugar
> 2 tablespoons lemon juice

Blend until vegetables are finely cut; chill until mixture begins to thicken, then add

> 1 9-ounce can crushed pineapple

Turn into large ring mold and chill until firm. Unmold on greens and serve with mayonnaise.

Frozen Roquefort Salad with Fruit

(8 to 12 portions)

Perfect with fresh or canned peaches or pears.

Whip in blender and place in a bowl

> 1 cup heavy cream

Without rinsing blender top, place in it

> ½ cup mayonnaise (p. 269)
> 8-ounce package softened cream cheese
> 2 small portions Roquefort cheese

Blend until smooth, mix with the whipped cream and freeze in tiny paper containers or in a layer about 1 inch thick. Serve portions with fruit, on lettuce.

Roquefort Ring

(8 servings)

Definitely a party girl!

Whip in blender on low speed and turn into a bowl

> 1 cup heavy cream

Place in blender top

> 1 tablespoon plain gelatin
> ¼ cup hot white wine

Blend to dissolve. Add

> ¼ cup more wine
> 2 tablespoons lemon juice
> ½ cup mayonnaise
> 1 thin slice onion
> ½ teaspoon worcestershire sauce
> 1 cup crumbled Roquefort or blue cheese
> 1 3-ounce package cream cheese (soft)

Blend until smooth. Fold in the cream and

> Salt and celery salt to taste

Turn into oiled 1-quart ring mold. Chill until firm. Unmold on watercress, romaine or other greens and fill the center of the ring with fresh fruit. Serve with Basic French Dressing (page 255).

Sauerkraut Salad or Relish

(8 servings)

Good with a ham or corned beef dinner.

Chop in blender separately

> 2 medium onions, quartered
> 1 green pepper, cut in pieces
> 5 6-inch pieces celery, cut in inch slices

Stir with fork into these ingredients, in a bowl

> 1 can (1 pound) sauerkraut, drained
> 3 tablespoons vinegar
> ½ cup sugar

Chill in covered container overnight before serving.

Salad Luncheon

(8 large molds or 1 loaf)

Hot rolls are all you need with this delicious salad.

Place in blender container

> 1 tablespoon plain gelatin
> 1 cup hot water

Blend a few seconds and add

> 1 avocado, peeled, seed removed
> 1 cup diced celery
> ½ cup mayonnaise
> 1 teaspoon salt
> 1 slice onion
> 2 tablespoons lemon juice

Blend until celery is finely chopped. Chill until slightly thickened and fold in

> 1 cup diced cooked corned beef or ham
> ¼ cup diced pimiento
> ¼ cup diced green pepper
> 2 diced hard-cooked eggs
> 2 cups cooked macaroni

Chill in individual 5-ounce molds or loaf pan until firm. Unmold on greens.

Sardine Stuffed Egg Salad

(4 servings)

Just fancy deviled eggs.

Hard cook

4 eggs

Cut lengthwise into halves and put yolks into blender container with

1 thin slice small onion
⅓ teaspoon salt
¼ teaspoon pepper
2 tablespoons chili sauce
2 tablespoons mayonnaise
2 sardines
2 or 3 slices cucumber
1 slice green pepper (optional)

Blend until ingredients are finely chopped. Pile filling into egg whites. Chill and serve on lettuce with Basic French Dressing (page 255).

Shrimp Party Salad

(6 or more servings)

A general favorite.

Place in blender top

2 tablespoons plain gelatin
1 cup hot water

Blend a few seconds and add

1½ cups chicken or fish broth
¼ cup lemon juice
½ teaspoon salt
1 cup mayonnaise (page 269)

Blend a few seconds and turn a little of the mixture into a ring mold to form a thin jellied layer. Arrange a few split whole shrimps and strips of pimiento in it in an attractive pattern. Chill until firm. Meanwhile, add to blender

> 1 cup cooked shrimps
> 1 cup diced celery
> 1 slice onion
> ¼ cup parsley
> 1 pimiento

Blend until ingredients are chopped fairly fine. Turn into ring mold on top of jellied layer and chill until firm. Unmold on a serving platter and garnish with greens. Serve with mayonnaise seasoned with a little lemon juice.

Glorified Tomato Aspic

(6 servings)

Just a little crunchiness—it's pleasant.

Place in blender container

> 1 package lemon gelatin
> 1 cup hot tomato juice

Blend a few seconds to dissolve gelatin. Add

> ¾ cup more tomato juice
> 2 tablespoons vinegar
> 1 thin slice onion
> 1 cup diced celery
> ¼ cup stuffed olives

Blend a few seconds to chop celery fairly fine. Add and blend until barely chopped

> 1 hard-cooked egg, quartered

Turn into individual molds (or 1 large one) and chill until firm. Unmold on greens and serve with mayonnaise.

9

Salad Dressings

Salad dressings are so easy and so perfectly emulsified in a blender that they're fun to make, and it's nothing at all to have 6 or more different kinds on hand, neatly labeled and stored in fruit jars or bottles, to use as your fancy chooses.

Reach for the Anchovy and Roquefort, or the Celery Seed Dressing; pick a sour-cream blend for the coleslaw, a garlicky sauce for a bowl of mixed greens.

Make big batches of Basic French Dressing and Mayonnaise. With these two you can have a hundred adventures in salad-making. Add ingredients as you please—onion and garlic, chili sauce and lemon juice, capers and anchovies, cheese and parsley and watercress. You can have everything dispersed so finely in your dressing that nothing can be identified except by flavor. But if you want a salad dressing with chopped egg or onion in it, you can have that kind, too, by switching on and off repeatedly or blending for only a few seconds on high speed.

For most dressings, everything goes into the blender container at once. You put the cover on, rest your hand lightly on top, switch on the motor and let it run for just a few seconds. Then empty the container into the jar you wish to store the dressing in.

My favorite dressings are included in this collection. I hope they'll be your favorites, too.

FRENCH DRESSINGS AND VARIATIONS

This good Basic French Dressing can be varied in dozens of ways, so make a big batch while you're at it, and add other ingredients to parts of the dressing to suit your fancy.

Basic French Dressing

(1 pint)

Take off from here in any direction!

½ cup vinegar
1½ cups salad oil
1½ teaspoons salt
2 teaspoons sugar
1 slice small onion
½ teaspoon paprika
½ teaspoon mustard

Whirl in the electric blender until emulsified, ½ minute or so, and store in a covered jar in the refrigerator.

Blue Cheese Dressing

To a cup of the Basic French Dressing add ¼ pound blue cheese. Or use Roquefort (French), Gorgonzola (Italian), Stilton (English), or the Danish blue cheese—the sharper the better. Blend until perfectly smooth, or let there be lumps, as you please.

Chutney Dressing

This is for meat salads—or for chicken or shrimp. Add as much as ¼ cup of chutney to a cup of the basic dressing. Don't blend until perfectly smooth; leave it a little bumpy.

Ginger Dressing

A cup of Basic French (*parlez-vous?*) plus 1 tablespoon preserved ginger and sirup. Good on fruits.

Lorenzo Dressing

Adds color to a salad.

> 1 cup Basic French Dressing
> 3 tablespoons chili sauce
> 2 or 3 green onions with tops, cut in pieces
> ¼ bunch watercress
> ½ pimiento

Blend until cress is finely chopped. Try this on French endive, chilled fresh asparagus, or canned pears.

Mint Dressing

Tuck about 6 sprigs of fresh mint into the blender with a cup of the Basic French Dressing (page 255) and let the motor run until the mint is in very fine particles. If for fruit salads, add a teaspoon of sugar, too.

Pecan Dressing

Subtly different, and so intriguing!

Sauté ¼ cup pecans in a little butter until browned lightly, and put into the blender for a whirl with 1 cup Basic French Dressing. Mixed greens take to this and vice versa. Perfect harmony!

Vinaigrette Dressing

(Around a cupful)

The perfect choice for asparagus.

1 cup Basic French Dressing or any good bottled
  one
6 stuffed olives
1 teaspoon capers
3 or 4 green onions with tops, cut in pieces
2 tablespoons pickle relish
3 or 4 sprigs parsley
1 teaspoon chervil (if you have it)

Blend until emulsified, not until perfectly smooth.

OTHER FRENCH-TYPE DRESSINGS

Anchovy French Dressing

(A little over 1 cup)

Perfection for mixed greens.

1 small tin (2 ounces) anchovy fillets or rolled anchovies with capers
¼ teaspoon salt
1 cup olive oil
1 teaspoon mustard
1 slice medium-sized onion
¼ cup vinegar (tarragon is good)

Use the oil in the anchovy can as well as the fish. Blend
everything for a minute or so, until you get a smooth dressing
which doesn't show its anchovy. (You can certainly *taste*
anchovy, though!) Some people like a little more vinegar for
extra sharpness—use ⅓ cup if you like. I usually make a
double batch of the anchovy dressing, we like it so much. It
improves on standing.

Anchovy and Beet Dressing

To the dressing above or to 1 cup Basic French Dressing add
¼ cup cooked diced beets and 2 quartered hard-cooked
eggs. If you use basic dressing, you'll have to add the an-

chovies, naturally—6 or 8. Then blend until smooth, or just until beets, eggs, and anchovies are chopped as you wish.

Anchovy and Roquefort Dressing

(Little over 1 cup)

Everybody raves over this!

⅔ cup olive oil or salad oil
1 can (2 ounces) anchovies with their oil
3 tablespoons vinegar
3 tablespoons lemon juice
1 sliver garlic
½ teaspoon each: mustard, sugar, onion salt, celery
salt
Dash worcestershire
Dash tabasco
3-ounce wedge Roquefort cheese
¼ teaspoon paprika

Blend until perfectly smooth.

Chiffonade Dressing

(1¼ cups)

Bright with beets.

¾ cup salad oil
¼ cup tarragon vinegar
½ teaspoon salt
1 teaspoon sugar
¼ teaspoon paprika
2 thin slices medium-sized onion
4 leafy sprigs parsley
1 hard-cooked egg, quartered
2 medium-sized beets, in pieces

Blend until the solids are in tiny pieces—chopped, rather than completely blended. This will take not much more than a switch-on, switch-off action of the motor.

Curry Dressing

(About 1 cup)

For meats, chicken, seafood, vegetable salads.

> 1 teaspoon salt
> 1 teaspoon curry powder
> 1 teaspoon sugar
> 1 slice medium-sized onion
> 3 or 4 sprigs parsley
> Thin sliver garlic
> 2-inch strip pared outer rind of lemon
> ¾ cup oil
> ¼ cup vinegar
> Dash cayenne pepper
> 1¼ teaspoons black pepper

Blend until smooth. You know how curry and chutney go to-gether—well, you can add 2 tablespoons chutney to this for a wonderfully good variation.

Russian Dressing

(About 3 cups)

Equally good on fruits or crisp vegetables.

> 1 can (8 ounces) tomato sauce
> ½ cup tarragon vinegar
> 2 teaspoons salt
> ½ teaspoon paprika
> 1 tablespoon worcestershire sauce
> 1 cup salad oil
> ¼ cup sugar
> ½ teaspoon pepper
> ½ teaspoon mustard
> Small clove garlic
> Small onion, quartered
> 3 tablespoons horseradish

Blend ingredients into a smooth emulsion.

Superb French Dressing

(3 cups)

This won a prize.

> 1 cup catsup
> ¼ cup sugar
> ½ cup vinegar (herb-flavored is nice)
> 1 teaspoon salt
> 1 small onion, quartered
> ½ teaspoon celery seed
> ¼ teaspoon paprika
> ¾ cup salad oil or olive oil, or ½ each

Give these ingredients a blending of about 30 seconds.

Wine Dressing

(1¼ cups)

For fruits or greens.

> 1 teaspoon salt
> 1 teaspoon sugar
> ¼ teaspoon dry mustard
> Dash pepper
> 1 slice medium-sized onion
> ½ cup white table wine
> ¼ cup white wine vinegar
> 1 cup salad oil

Blend until emulsified.

Red Wine Dressing

(About 1½ cups)

For that big bowl of mixed greens and tomatoes.

> 1 teaspoon sugar
> 1 teaspoon salt

½ teaspoon mustard
1 teaspoon worcestershire sauce
¼ cup catsup
¼ cup red table wine
¼ cup red wine vinegar
1 cup olive oil
1 clove garlic

Blend until perfectly smooth.

FRUIT SALAD DRESSINGS AND DRESSINGS MADE WITH FRUITS

Dressings for fruit salads usually are sweeter than those for vegetable salads, mixed greens and the hearty salads made with meat, fish or chicken. Most of them are attractive in appearance, too, whether color or texture is the distinguishing quality.

Avocado Dressing

(1 cup or thereabouts)

For tomato salads, citrus fruits or greens.

1 large ripe avocado, peeled and pitted
¼ small onion
1 medium-sized tomato, quartered
3 tablespoons lemon juice
1 tablespoon olive oil
1 teaspoon salt
¼ teaspoon pepper
Dash tabasco

Blend until smooth. Lemon protects the color of avocado. You can even use more and counteract any sourness or sharpness with a little sugar. Put in a whole pared lemon, if you like, cutting it in pieces first and removing seeds. One lemon is the equivalent, in general, of 3 tablespoons juice.

Celery Seed Dressing

(1 pint)

Sweet and transparent-looking; the best of its kind, I think.

⅔ cup sugar
1½ teaspoons salt
1 tablespoon paprika
½ teaspoon mustard
½ cup tarragon wine vinegar
¼ medium-sized onion
1 cup salad oil
1 tablespoon or more celery seed

Blend until thick and smooth.

Sesame Seed Dressing

Use the same recipe, substituting toasted sesame seeds for celery. Toast the seeds in a small pan over moderate heat, shaking the pan to prevent scorching, and heating only until they look pale gold.

Cranberry Cream Dressing

(More than a cup)

A pale pink.

Boil for 5 minutes

⅔ cup fresh cranberries
3 tablespoons sugar
2 tablespoons water
½ teaspoon salt

Cool and put in blender with

3 tablespoons salad oil
1½ tablespoons lemon juice

Fold into

>   ⅓ cup cream, whipped until thick

Cream Cheese and Currant Dressing

(About 2 cups)

"Elegant!" you'll say.

>   ½ cup currant jelly
>   3-ounce package cream cheese
>   3 tablespoons lemon juice
>   ¼ teaspoon salt

Blend until smooth. Then fold in

>   1 cup whipped cream
>   3 tablespoons blender-chopped nuts

French Fruit Dressing

(About 1½ cups)

Lime juice is the secret.

>   ½ cup lime juice
>   About 1 square inch outer peel of lime
>   ¼ teaspoon worcestershire
>   ¼ teaspoon mustard
>   ¼ teaspoon salt
>   ¼ teaspoon paprika
>   ⅓ cup sugar
>   1 cup salad oil

Blend until smooth. So good with melon salads and fruit-salad plates!

Golden French Dressing

(About 1½ cups)

Serve this with a fruit-salad plate.

> 1 cup salad oil
> Juice 1 orange
> Juice 1 lemon
> Small piece outer rind of both orange and lemon
> ½ cup sugar
> 1 tablespoon vinegar
> ½ teaspoon salt
> 1 teaspoon paprika

Blend until smooth.

Spring Salad Dressing

(Around a pint)

As good for mixed greens as for fruit salads.

> 1 peeled seeded grapefruit, in pieces
> ½ cup salad oil
> 3 tablespoons tarragon vinegar
> 1 tablespoon sugar
> 1 teaspoon prepared mustard
> 1 teaspoon paprika
> ½ teaspoon salt
> 3 tablespoons catsup
> 1 small onion, quartered
> 1 lemon, pared and seeded, in quarters

Blend until smooth.

CREAM, SOUR CREAM AND OTHER DAIRY
FOOD DRESSINGS

Cottage cheese converts to sour-cream texture in a blender, and if calories are a problem, you couldn't do better. Add a tablespoon or two of lemon juice and some salt and pepper to use cottage cheese as a dressing by itself.

Buttermilk Blue Cheese Dressing

(About 2½ cups)

The tart flavor of buttermilk comes through enticingly.

Place in blender container

> 1 cup buttermilk
> 6 ounces blue cheese
> 1 sliver garlic
> 6 green onions with tops, cut in 1-inch pieces
> ½ teaspoon salt
> 5 or 6 sprigs parsley

Blend until cheese and vegetables are fine. Add and blend just to mix

> 1 cup mayonnaise or salad dressing

Flavors blend better upon standing. Try to make the dressing a day before you use it.

Coleslaw Cream Dressing

(About 2 cups)

You could serve this with ham, as a sauce.

> 1 cup whipping cream
> 1 egg
> 2 tablespoons horseradish
> 2 teaspoons prepared mustard
> 1 teaspoon salt
> ½ teaspoon sugar
> ¼ teaspoon paprika
> 2 tablespoons lemon juice

Blend until thick and smooth.

Cottage Cheese Dressing with Buttermilk

(About 1 cup)

Beloved by weight-watchers.

½ cup cottage cheese
½ cup buttermilk
¼ cup lemon juice
1 teaspoon salt
½ teaspoon paprika
3 hard-cooked egg yolks
Sliver garlic
½ green pepper, cut in pieces
4 radishes

Blend until green pepper and radishes are finely chopped, not until they are minced too fine to show in the dressing. Awfully good on greens.

Dairy Garden Dressing

(More than 3 cups)

Marvelous on greens.

1 carton (1 pound) cottage cheese
1 carton (8 ounces) sour cream
1 teaspoon salt
¼ teaspoon white pepper
1 tablespoon lemon or lime juice
½ cucumber, in chunks
6 green onions with tops, cut in 1-inch slices
6 radishes
1 strip green pepper
Few sprigs parsley

Blend everything until vegetables are chopped, not too fine. Garden herbs could be added.

Quick Sour Cream Dressing

(A little over a cup)

Try it on cucumbers and tomato salad.

> 1 cup sour cream
> ¼ cup lemon juice
> 2 tablespoons sugar
> 1 teaspoon salt
> Dash cayenne
> Sprig of parsley (optional)

Blend until smooth and fluffy and use to dress vegetable or fruit salads. Don't over-blend. Sour cream may break down if you do.

Sour Cream Horseradish Dressing

(About 2 cups)

Sharp, but refreshing!

> 1 cup sour cream
> ¼ cup fresh prepared horseradish
> ½ cup catsup
> 2 tablespoons salad oil
> 2 tablespoons vinegar or lemon juice
> 2 tablespoons sugar
> 1 teaspoon salt

Beat in the blender until smooth. Good on coleslaw and fish salads, especially. Also fine for greens.

Sour Cream Shrimp Dressing

(About 2 cups)

Lobster or crabmeat is good in it, too.

> 1 cup sour cream
> 1 thin sliver garlic

¼ cup catsup
1 tablespoon worcestershire
1 slice medium-sized onion
1 tablespoon horseradish
1 tablespoon lemon juice
½ teaspoon salt
¼ teaspoon mustard
½ teaspoon paprika
¼ pound cooked or canned shrimp

Blend smooth and serve on crisp greens.

Yogurt Dressing

(Little over a cupful)

Tangy, delicious and low-caloried.

1 cup yogurt
1 teaspoon sugar
½ teaspoon salt
Dash pepper
¼ teaspoon mustard
¼ teaspoon paprika
2 tablespoons chili sauce or catsup

Whirl in the blender until thoroughly combined.

MAYONNAISE AND SIMILAR DRESSINGS

The mayonnaise you make in the blender is the smoothest, fluffiest, most wonderful stuff. And it's perfectly emulsified in nothing flat! Mayonnaise is the base of innumerable fine dressings in addition to being an excellent one all by itself, and many fine sauces for meat and fish begin with a mayonnaise base. Some of them are included here since they function as dressing or sauce equally well.

Mayonnaise

(A pint or so)

You'll make this a thousand times.

Put into the blender container

>1 egg
>1 teaspoon salt
>1 teaspoon sugar
>1 teaspoon mustard
>½ teaspoon paprika
>3 tablespoons vinegar or lemon juice

Cover, switch on the motor for just a few seconds, then uncover and add gradually, with the motor running

>1½ cups salad oil (less if mixture thickens quickly)

Blend only until very thick and smooth.

Almond Mayonnaise: Add 2 tablespoons lemon juice and ¼ cup Almond Paste (page 354) to 1 cup mayonnaise and blend.

Sauce Verte: Add 1 clove garlic, 1 bunch parsley, dash tabasco. Blend green and smooth. Lush!

Caviar Dressing

(A little over a cup)

Don't use the best caviar for this—it's good with the cheapest!

>1 cup mayonnaise, above
>1 small rib celery with tops
>1 pimiento
>½ green pepper, in pieces
>½ small onion
>2 tablespoons lemon juice
>3 drops tabasco sauce

Blend until smooth. Stir in

> 1 tablespoon red or black caviar

This can double as a sauce for fish and seafood.

Cranberry Mayonnaise

(1½ cups)

Pale pink and perfect for fruit salads.

> ½ cup cooked or canned cranberry sauce
> ½ cup mayonnaise (page 269)
> ½ cup sour cream

Blend until smooth. You could spike it with horseradish, but it's very nice as is. Can be used as a fish sauce.

Cucumber Dressing

(Around 1½ cups)

Fine for cold salmon.

> 1 cup mayonnaise (page 269)
> 2 tablespoons chili sauce
> 1 tablespoon vinegar
> ½ teaspoon salt
> ¼ teaspoon pepper
> 6 pitted green olives or 6 stuffed olives
> 1 rib celery, cut up, with tops
> 1 cucumber, unpared, in pieces

Blend until solid ingredients are chopped fairly fine, but not until you get a smooth sauce. This is good with greens, vegetable salads or as a sauce for cold fish.

Ever-So-Good Dressing

(Nearly a quart)

Something like Thousand Island, good on any salad.

2 cups mayonnaise (recipe on page 269 or commercial)
1 cup chili sauce
2 hard-cooked eggs, quartered
3 or 4 gherkins
1 medium onion, quartered
1 pimiento
½ green pepper, in chunks
4 pieces celery about 6 inches long, cut in 1-inch pieces

Blend just until eggs and vegetables are chopped.

Green Goddess Dressing

(A "heaping" pint)

Good on seafood or greens.

1 cup mayonnaise (page 269)
1 clove garlic
4 anchovies
6 green onions with tops, cut in pieces
¼ cup parsley, packed in cup
1 tablespoon lemon juice
1 tablespoon tarragon vinegar
½ teaspoon salt
¼ teaspoon coarse-ground pepper

Blend until anchovies, onions and parsley are in fine particles. Mix with sour or sweet whipped cream to serve.

Lamaze Dressing or Sauce

(More than a pint)

Almost a relish.

1 cup mayonnaise (page 269)
1 cup chili sauce or catsup
¼ cup piccalilli or India relish

1 pimiento
1 rib celery, cut in pieces
1 slice green pepper
1 slice onion
1 tablespoon worcestershire sauce
1 teaspoon mustard

Blend until solids are in fine particles. My family loves this mixed with yogurt or sour cream, on green salad. It's an elegant sauce for cold salmon and other fish, too.

Parisian Dressing

(1 pint)

Sophisticated.

½ teaspoon mustard
½ teaspoon salt
Dash white pepper
¼ cup red-wine vinegar
1 egg
2 green onions, with tops, in pieces
Thin sliver garlic
2 hard-cooked egg yolks
½ bunch watercress

Blend about 30 seconds, then add gradually

1½ cups salad oil

Blend to smooth, thick emulsion.

Roquefort Mayonnaise

(Around a cupful)

For chicken and fish salads, mostly.

1 cup mayonnaise (page 269)
⅓ cup Roquefort or blue cheese
1 medium-sized pickle, cut up
6 stuffed olives

5 or 6 sprigs parsley
1 tablespoon lemon juice
Dash tabasco sauce

Blend until mixed, but leave fine pieces.

Thousand Island Dressing

(1 pint)

For head lettuce, chicken.

1 cup mayonnaise (page 269)
¼ cup chili sauce or catsup
1 slice onion
¾ cup diced celery
¼ cup stuffed olives
¼ cup sweet pickle relish
2 or 3 sprigs parsley
1 slice green pepper
1 hard-cooked egg, quartered
1 teaspoon paprika

Blend, but not until smooth. Solids should only be chopped.

COOKED SALAD DRESSINGS

The procedure for cooked dressings is to blend first, then cook. Such dressings are smooth as can be.

Old-Fashioned Cooked Dressing

(1½ cups)

Better than grandma's!

2 tablespoons flour
1½ teaspoons salt
1 teaspoon mustard
2 tablespoons sugar
¼ teaspoon paprika

> 1 egg
> 1¼ cups milk
> ⅓ cup vinegar

Blend thoroughly, pour into saucepan and cook over hot water until thick. Stir while cooking. Add

> 1 tablespoon butter

Coleslaw Dressing

(1 pint)

Good on any greens.

> 2 eggs
> ½ cup sugar
> 1½ teaspoons salt
> ⅛ teaspoon pepper
> 1 cup sweet or sour cream
> ½ cup vinegar
> 1 teaspoon celery seed

Blend smooth, then cook in a double boiler to smooth custard.

Golden Dressing

(About 1 pint)

For fruit salads.

> ¼ cup sirup from canned fruit (peaches, pears, pine-
> apple)
> ¼ cup orange juice
> 2 tablespoons lemon juice
> ¼ teaspoon salt
> ¼ teaspoon dry mustard
> Few grains cayenne pepper
> 2 eggs
> ½ cup sugar

Blend smooth, then cook in the top of a double boiler until custardy, stirring constantly.

10 | Sauces Smooth as Silk

It's extinct—that lumpy white sauce. It's gone—that bumpy gravy. The electric blender prevents the formation of lumps by perfectly combining liquid and thickener, and it magically unlumps a ruffian sauce made carelessly the old way.

Blend first, then cook, is the general rule. It's a time-saving, sure method. Here's just one example of the new speed and efficiency with which you can prepare a dish: for scalloped potatoes, blend milk, flour, seasonings, and pour over the sliced potatoes, without the step of cooking the sauce until thickened. It thickens as the casserole bakes, and with nary a lump or curdle.

WHITE OR CREAM SAUCE
AND SOME VARIATIONS

Medium White Sauce

(1 cup)

Use this for all creamed dishes.

      1 cup milk
      2 tablespoons flour

½ teaspoon salt
Dash of pepper

Blend ingredients smooth and pour over dish to be baked; or turn into a saucepan and cook, stirring constantly until thickened. Add (unless you are counting calories or cutting down on fat)

2 tablespoons butter

Thick or Thin Sauce

Thick White Sauce is used as the base for croquettes and meat, fish, chicken or vegetable rings, sometimes with the addition of eggs. It also is the base of most soufflés. It is the glue that sticks these things together, and it is very simply made in the blender by just increasing the flour to double the amount—4 tablespoons. Almost always, you'll want to turn the mixture into a saucepan, then, and cook it by itself until thickened. Thin White Sauce is the base for cream soups, and it is made by cutting the flour in half—1 tablespoon of flour to a cup of milk.

Caper Sauce for Fish

Blend an egg yolk with Medium White Sauce and cook and stir until thickened. Then add 1 tablespoon capers and 1 teaspoon lemon juice.

Onion, Parsley and Pimiento Sauce

Blend a slice of onion, 2 or 3 sprigs of parsley, a drained pimiento with the Medium White Sauce. Wonderful for vegetables, cooked chicken or fish.

Good Gravy

There are two kinds of gravy: (1) pan gravy, which is simply drippings from meat which has been broiled, pan-broiled or roasted, minus excess fat and plus enough water to loosen the good meat particles that have browned and attached themselves to the pan, and (2) thickened meat gravy which is simply a white sauce made with water in place of milk. For each cup of thickened gravy put 2 tablespoons flour and a cup of water into the blender, give the mixture a fast whirl and turn into the pan drippings after removing excess fat. If the drippings are good and brown, you'll get brown gravy without browning the flour—and the blender method is antilump. Also, it enables you to cut down on the fat in your gravy if you wish. The old way, you had to use 2 tablespoons fat to 2 tablespoons flour to get a solid foundation for your gravy.

Giblet Gravy

(3 cups)

Giblets are easily chopped in the blender for gravy or stuffing.

Simmer until tender

> Giblets and neck of chicken, turkey or other bird
> 1 onion
> 1 rib celery
> Salt, pepper
> 1 quart water (more for turkey parts which are large)

Take out liver as soon as it is tender. Cool giblets in stock. Remove meat from neck bones. Cut up giblets.

Place in blender, in small amounts, with some of the stock. Chop as fine as you wish.

To make gravy, blend with a spoon in saucepan or skillet

> 6 tablespoons drippings from roasting fowl
> 6 tablespoons flour

Add

> 3 cups giblet cooking stock
> Salt, pepper to taste

Stir in chopped giblets and neck meat of chicken, about half the chopped turkey parts.* Cook and stir until thickened. If gravy is too thick, thin with more stock, or a little white wine.

* Either make twice as much gravy, use remaining giblets in stuffing or freeze for another time.

SOME SAUCES FOR MEATS, FISH, POULTRY AND VEGETABLES

For some others, see Mayonnaise and Similar Dressings, pages 268-273, and Entrees, pages 194-235.

Almond Butter Sauce

(⅔ cup or so)

This is the "amandine" for the fish, or for asparagus or green beans.

Sauté in

> ½ cup butter
> ¼ cup split blanched almonds

When golden brown, place in blender and chop with

> 1 tablespoon lemon juice

Barbecue Sauce

(1½ cups)

Just spicy enough.

Quarter, then sauté

> 1 medium-sized onion in
> ½ cup butter or margarine

Turn into the blender container and add

> 1 tablespoon prepared mustard
> ½ cup vinegar

1 tablespoon worcestershire sauce
1-inch square outer peel of lemon
¼ cup chili sauce
2 tablespoons brown sugar
1 teaspoon salt
¼ teaspoon pepper

Blend until onion is finely chopped. Use to baste meat or chicken during roasting. Sauce can be "hottened" with tabasco sauce, but be cautious.

Lazy-C Ranch Barbecue Sauce

(About 3½ cups)

A good outdoors recipe for beef, lamb, chicken or fish.

Place in blender container

2 or 3 cloves garlic
2 medium onions, quartered
½ lemon, cut in quarters
¼ cup lemon juice
1 tablespoon prepared mustard
2 tablespoons horseradish
5 or 6 sprigs parsley
1 teaspoon black pepper
2 teaspoons chili powder
¼ cup sugar
½ cup catsup
1 teaspoon salt
1 teaspoon tabasco sauce
1 cup water

Blend until ingredients are chopped fine, then pour into saucepan with

2 cups bouillon
1 cup oil

Simmer together for an hour, stirring occasionally. Spoon or brush over meat being cooked on rotisserie or outdoor grill, or over roast prepared in an oven.

Barbecue Sauce for Spareribs

(More than 2 cups)

A good sauce for roast pork on the rotisserie, too.

Sauté in ¼ cup oil

2 large onions, sliced

Place in blender container with

1 cup catsup
½ cup molasses, honey or brown sugar
2 tablespoons prepared mustard
½ cup vinegar
1 teaspoon salt
1 teaspoon chili powder, optional
¼ teaspoon black pepper (or more)

Blend until onions are finely chopped. Heat in saucepan and use to baste meat as it cooks.

Cantonese Sweet-Sour Sauce

(About 1 cup)

A piquant dressing for shrimps, ham, pork or duck.

½ cup cooked dried, or drained canned apricots
A few pieces candied or preserved ginger
½ cup vinegar
½ cup sugar

Blend until ginger is chopped. Use very little ginger or as much as a tablespoonful, depending upon how hot you want the sauce. A teaspoon of mustard or horseradish mustard may also be added.

Seafood Cocktail Sauce

(About 2 cups)

One of the best!

Place in blender container

> Outer peel of ½ lemon
> Juice of 2 lemons (about 6 tablespoons)
> 2 teaspoons worcestershire sauce
> 1 teaspoon (less, if you wish) tabasco sauce
> 1 tablespoon horseradish
> ½ onion, cut in two
> 1 clove garlic
> 1 rib celery, with tops, cut in inch pieces

Blend until ingredients are cut fine, then fold in

> 1 cup mayonnaise (p. 269)
> Salt and coarse black pepper as needed

Chill and serve with any kind of seafood.

Jiffy Cheese Sauce

(2 cups)

Extraordinary!

> 1 can condensed cream-of-celery soup
> ⅓ cup white table wine
> ½ pound cheddar cheese, in cubes
> ½ teaspoon worcestershire sauce
> 2 tablespoons flour
> Salt, pepper

Blend smooth and stir over low heat until thoroughly hot and thickened. Serve over vegetables or over poached eggs.

Creole Sauce for Fish, Meat or Vegetables

(1 pint)

The Spanish cook's stand-by.

Dice and cook for 5 minutes

> 1 medium-sized onion
> ½ green pepper in
> ¼ cup butter or margarine

Put in blender with

> 1½ cups canned tomatoes
> 1 sliver garlic
> 1 teaspoon salt
> 1 teaspoon sugar
> Dash of black pepper

Blend until vegetables are chopped. Don't overdo this and make them too fine. Heat and serve with fish or other food. Shrimp, frozen fillets of almost any fish are especially good in this sauce. It can be more highly seasoned if you like.

Cucumber Lemon Sauce

(1½ cups)

Pale green and so refreshing!

> 2 medium-sized cucumbers, cut in pieces
>   (don't pare)
> Juice of 1 lemon
> 1 teaspoon salt
> ¼ teaspoon paprika

Blend until cucumber is finely grated. Good with fish. Sauce can be combined with mayonnaise (page 269) or sour cream if you wish.

Cumberland Sauce for Duck or Chicken

(1 cup)

Perfect poultry partner.

> Outer peel of 1 orange, in pieces
> ½ cup currant jelly
> ¼ cup port wine
> ¼ cup orange juice
> 2 tablespoons lemon juice
> 2 teaspoons dry mustard

      1 teaspoon paprika
      ½ teaspoon ground ginger
      1 teaspoon cornstarch

Blend until orange rind is finely cut, pour into saucepan and simmer, stirring constantly, for 5 minutes.

Garlic Sauce

(About ⅔ cup)

Gives hamburgers or steaks a snap.

      1 clove garlic
      2 tablespoons butter
      ¼ cup catsup
      ¼ cup vinegar
      1 tablespoon worcestershire sauce
      1 teaspoon paprika
      ½ teaspoon dry mustard
      2 drops tabasco sauce

Blend about 20 seconds and serve with meat.

Gingersnap Sauce

(1½ cups)

For ham, tongue or pot roast.

Place in blender

      5 gingersnaps
      1 slice onion
      ½ cup brown sugar
      1 cup hot water
      1 thick slice lemon

Blend smooth; turn into saucepan and add

      ¼ cup raisins
      ¼ cup vinegar

Cook until thickened.

Hollandaise Sauce

(1½ cups)

Nothing like it for green vegetables!

2 eggs
½ teaspoon salt
2 tablespoons lemon juice
½ cup soft butter
Dash of white pepper (or black)
1 thin slice onion (optional)
Sliver garlic (optional)

Blend until smooth, and with motor running, add gradually

½ cup hot water

Blend smooth again and then cook over hot water, stirring constantly, to custard consistency. Can be served hot or cold over vegetables. Blend a handful of spinach or watercress with this for green hollandaise—wonderful with fish.

Happiness Hollandaise

(¾ cup)

How to dress the asparagus quickly and with no curdle!

Melt, just to bubbling (do not brown)

1 stick (¼ pound) sweet (unsalted) butter

Place in blender container

3 egg yolks
2 tablespoons lemon juice
½ teaspoon salt
Dash tabasco sauce

Cover; turn blender on and off once. Then turn to high speed and quickly pour in hot butter, in a steady stream. Turn off motor. Sauce will be emulsified. Keep it warm in a double boiler over low heat, or refrigerate to heat as needed. If sauce thickens, re-blend it, adding 1 to 2 tablespoons hot water, or more lemon juice.

Perfect for eggs benedict (poached eggs on fried ham slices on toast or toasted English muffin halves).

Whipped Cream Horseradish Sauce

(About 1½ cups)

Delightful with cold sliced ham or turkey.

Whip in blender and place in bowl

>   1 cup heavy cream

Mince in blender with ¼ cup water, then drain

>   4 or 5 sprigs parsley

Fold drained parsley into whipped cream with

>   ¼ teaspoon salt
>   ½ cup horseradish

Chill sauce before serving. Parsley may be omitted if you prefer a snowy sauce.

Lemon Garlic Sauce

(1½ cups)

For fish and seafood, or salads made with them.

>   2 small cloves garlic
>   1 teaspoon salt
>   ½ cup salad oil
>   1 cup lemon juice
>   1 medium onion, quartered
>   1 teaspoon thyme
>   ½ teaspoon pepper

Whirl sauce until smooth in blender.

Quick Mint Sauce for Lamb

(About 1 cup)

All you need is fresh mint!

> ½ bunch fresh, washed mint (or a handful!)
> ¼ cup sugar
> 1 cup hot vinegar

Blend until mint is chopped fairly fine. Serve hot or cold. Keep what's left in a covered jar. Flavor develops as it stands.

French Mustard

(About 1 cup)

You can't make it too hot for a mustard lover! Excellent with cold meats.

> 1 clove garlic
> 1 onion, quartered
> 1 cup wine vinegar
> 1 teaspoon salt
> Dash tabasco sauce
> ½ cup dry mustard
> 2 tablespoons olive oil
> 1 teaspoon tarragon

Blend ingredients together until smooth. Store in covered jar to use as wanted.

Olive Sauce

(4 servings)

Serve hot with veal or fish.

> 2 tablespoons butter
> 1 cup beef bouillon
> 1 tablespoon sugar

½ teaspoon each: salt, paprika
½ cup tomato sauce
¾ cup stuffed or pitted ripe olives
1 tablespoon lemon juice
1 slice onion
2 tablespoons flour

Blend ingredients until onion and olives are chopped fairly fine. Transfer to saucepan and simmer until thickened, stirring constantly.

Orange Sauce for Pork Chops

(Enough for 4)

Glaze, garnish and glamor.

Pared outer rind of 1 orange
½ cup orange juice
1½ teaspoons cornstarch
1 teaspoon sugar
1 tablespoon lemon juice

Blend until orange rind is fine, then transfer to saucepan and cook and stir until mixture thickens and clears. Add

1 thick slice orange, cut in quarters

Serve warm over braised or grilled pork chops.

Parsley Sauce for Broiled Steak

(About ½ cup)

This makes gourmet food of a good thick steak.

¼ cup packed parsley
1 tablespoon worcestershire sauce
½ teaspoon dry mustard
2 tablespoons melted butter
2 tablespoons water
Pared strip outer peel of lemon

Blend to cut very fine. After steak is broiled, transfer it to a hot platter, skim excess fat from the drippings, add this combination to drippings and bring to simmering. Pour over steak, seasoning well with salt and coarse black pepper.

Spaghetti Sauce with Wine

(Enough to serve 6)

Good on rice or noodles, too.

Sauté

> 2 onions, quartered, in
> ¼ cup olive oil

Turn into blender with

> 1 cup red wine
> 1 small can mushrooms
> 1 clove garlic

Blend until onion is finely chopped and turn into saucepan with

> 1 pound hamburger, browned in skillet after onions
> 1 cup more red wine
> 1 can (6 ounces) tomato paste
> 2 cups canned tomatoes
> ½ teaspoon basil or oregano
> 1½ teaspoons salt (more, if needed)
> ¼ teaspoon pepper

Simmer until sauce is heavy, about an hour.

Spaghetti Sauce for a Party

(8 to 12 servings)

Make it ahead and freeze it, if you wish.

Blender-chop, in small amounts, and empty into large skillet with ¼ cup oil in it

2 medium onions, quartered
2 green peppers, cut in pieces
4 carrots, sliced
6 ribs celery with tops, cut in 1-inch lengths
½ pound fresh mushrooms

Cook gently for 5 minutes with

1 or 2 cloves garlic, put through garlic press or crushed

Brown separately in 2 tablespoons more oil

1½ pounds ground beef

Add to the sautéed vegetables with

1 can (6 ounces) tomato paste
1 No. 2½ can (3½ cups) Italian pear tomatoes
1 tablespoon salt
½ teaspoon pepper
½ teaspoon oregano
1 tablespoon worcestershire sauce
1 tablespoon sugar
2 cups beef bouillon
1 cup red table wine

Cook at simmering, stirring now and then, for 2 hours, or until sauce cooks down and thickens. Serve over cooked spaghetti, macaroni, noodles or rice.

Helen's Tartar Sauce

(2 cups)

Delicious with corned beef hash as well as fish.

1 cup mayonnaise (p. 269)
1 teaspoon prepared mustard
1 teaspoon each: chervil, tarragon
2 dill pickles, cut in chunks
1 small onion, quartered
1 tablespoon capers

¼ cup lemon juice
½ teaspoon worcestershire sauce
Few drops tabasco sauce

Blend a few seconds, only until pickle and onion are chopped.

Watercress Sauce for Fish

(About 1¼ cups)

An attractive green sauce with the pepperiness of cress and the tartness of lemon.

1 cup mayonnaise (p. 269)
1 bunch watercress
1 tablespoon lemon juice
1 slice onion

Blend until cress and onion are chopped fine.

DESSERT SAUCES

Apricot or Peach Rum Sauce

(A little more than a pint)

Serve hot on steamed puddings; cold on angel cake.

1 No. 2½ can apricots or peaches, drained
¼ cup liquid from fruit
1 tablespoon lemon juice
⅓ cup sugar
1 tablespoon cornstarch
¼ teaspoon salt

Blend until fruit is puréed; pour into saucepan and cook, stirring constantly, until thickened and clear. Add

> ¼ cup light rum
> Few drops almond or vanilla extract
> 2 tablespoons butter (optional; omit if sauce is to be
> used cold)

Try this on Wonder Sponge Cake (page 88), hot on Plain Two-Egg Cake (page 84), cold on blanc mange, or on a good vanilla ice cream. Pretty fancy!

Brandy Hard Sauce

(Enough for 6 desserts)

The perfect topper for a Christmas pudding.

> 2 tablespoons brandy (or rum or sherry)
> ¼ teaspoon nutmeg
> ⅓ cup soft butter
> 1 cup confectioners' sugar

Blend until smooth.

Butterscotch Ice Cream Sauce

(About 1½ cups)

Best on vanilla.

Place in blender container

> 1 cup evaporated milk
> ¾ cup brown sugar
> ½ cup white sugar
> 2 tablespoons butter
> 1 tablespoon corn sirup
> Dash of salt
> ½ teaspoon vanilla

Blend smooth on high speed.

Rich, Thick Chocolate Sauce

(About 1¾ cups)

No cooking! Imagine!

> 4 squares unsweetened chocolate, cut in small
>   pieces
> 1 cup sugar
> ⅔ cup warm milk, cream, coffee or sherry
> 1 teaspoon vanilla
> Dash of salt

Blend until smooth. This is a luscious sauce. Use it for ice cream, pudding, for frosting a cake, flavoring malted milk. Keep it, if you can keep it at all, in the refrigerator. A wonderful church bazaar item.

Custard Sauce with Almonds

(Around a pint)

Nice on a date pudding.

> ½ cup milk
> ½ cup blanched almonds
> ¼ cup sugar
> Dash of salt

Blend until almonds are chopped. Add and blend just a second or two

> 2 eggs
> 1½ cups more milk

Pour into saucepan or double-boiler top and cook and stir over hot water until mixture will just coat a spoon. Add

> ¼ teaspoon almond extract

Chill immediately. Serve over plain cake, baked or steamed puddings.

Lemon Sauce

(1½ cups)

Your favorite and mine.

> ½ cup sugar
> 1 cup warm water
> 1 tablespoon cornstarch
> Dash of salt
> Dash of nutmeg
> Outer skin of ½ lemon
> Peeled ½ lemon

Blend until lemon peel is finely grated; pour into saucepan and cook, stirring constantly, until thickened and clear. Add

> 1 tablespoon butter

Serve warm on Plain Two-Egg Cake, page 84 (this combination makes cottage pudding), or on bread pudding or steamed pudding.

Mincemeat Brandy Sauce

(1½ cups)

Rich, dark and heavy.

> 1 cup canned mincemeat
> ¼ cup apple juice or orange juice
> ¼ cup brandy

Give these ingredients a nice whirl to make a smooth sauce which is delicious cold on ice cream, hot on puddings.

Orange Sauce

(1 cup)

A topping for cakes, soufflés and puddings.

> Pared outer rind of ½ orange
> ½ cup orange juice

½ cup sugar
¼ teaspoon salt
1 tablespoon cornstarch
2 tablespoons butter
1 tablespoon lemon juice
¾ cup hot water

Blend until orange rind is fine. Turn into saucepan and cook until thickened, stirring constantly. Serve warm.

Raisin Dessert Sauce

(Nearly 2 cups)

Sherry could replace ½ cup of the water.

Place in blender top

Rind (only yellow part) of ½ lemon
1½ cups water
¼ cup sugar
⅛ teaspoon salt
2 teaspoons cornstarch
2 tablespoons butter

Blend until lemon peel is very fine, add and blend just to chop

⅓ cup raisins

Heat to the boiling point, then simmer a few minutes. Serve warm or chilled on ice cream, custard or pudding.

Rum Butter Sauce

(About 2 cups)

Serve it over ice cream or fresh sliced peaches.

Whip in blender and set aside

1 cup heavy cream

Place in blender top

> ¼ cup sugar
> ⅛ teaspoon salt
> 1 egg
> 1 to 2 tablespoons rum or
>   2 teaspoons rum flavoring
> ⅓ cup melted butter

Blend until smooth, just a few seconds. Fold into the whipped cream. Keep in a covered jar in the refrigerator.

Peppermint Stick Sauce for Ice Cream

(1½ cups)

So good on chocolate!

Crush in blender container

> 12 peppermint sugar candy sticks

Add and blend on high speed

> ¾ cup heavy cream
> 4 marshmallows, quartered

Sauce may be a pretty pink!

Raspberry Sauce with Kirsch

(Around 1¼ cups)

Tee-rific!

> 12-ounce glass raspberry jelly
> ¼ cup kirsch or cherry brandy
> 3 or 4 slices outer rind of orange

Blend until rind is finely grated and sauce is smooth. This is potent but perfect for any number of desserts, particularly the light-colored ones (custard, blanc mange, Russian cream) where the light contrast as well as the flavor is interesting.

Strawberry Marshmallow Sauce

(Over a pint)

A pink fluff.

> 1 box (12-ounce) frozen strawberries, thawed
> slightly and broken up
> ¼ cup fruit juice or sirup from canned fruit
> ¼ pound marshmallows, quartered

Blend until smooth. Perfect as an ice-cream topping or parfait sauce.

11 | Soups

The Mock Turtle's soup of the evening could have been no richer and greener than the soup you can turn out of your blender, using peas or asparagus, broccoli, spinach or watercress. Purée any cooked vegetable in your blender, with milk or stock and a piece of onion, turn it into a saucepan, season and heat to the bubbling point. It's smooth, delicious soup, and no straining necessary! A cooked vegetable is its own thickener. You may need to dilute it with milk or stock, but you rarely need to thicken it.

You can make amazingly good soups with all the scraps from your refrigerator. This is a favorite trick of mine, and my family thinks each soup is better than the last. A dab of creamed dried beef, the leftover breakfast bacon, a hunk of mashed potatoes from last night, the little dish of corn and peas—swung together in the blender, with some onion, parsley and milk, these bits of perfectly good food that might otherwise be wasted become a substantial lunch. Blend, heat and eat! Was there ever a simpler recipe?

You can do wonderful things with canned and frozen soups, using your blender: Blend chilled tomato soup with half and half for a cold treat; whirl together a can of frozen oyster soup and a can of cream of celery, diluting with milk or milk and cream, and serve cold or hot. Frozen shrimp with cream of mushroom, canned pea and frozen potato—oh, well, YOU try it!

The Flavor Is Fresher

For really fresh flavor, start with a raw vegetable and chop it fine in the blender, with part of the liquid—milk or stock—you plan to use. Add thickening, too, since a chopped vegetable usually requires thickening. Cooking time for a soup made from a blender-chopped raw vegetable is very short, and thus the fresh flavor is preserved.

Pattern for a Cream Soup Made in the Blender

(2 servings)

Make it with one vegetable or a mixture.

> 1 cup diced raw vegetable
> 1 teaspoon salt
> Dash of pepper
> 2 tablespoons flour
> 2 cups milk
> 1 slice onion
> Sprig or 2 parsley (optional)

Blend until vegetable is chopped, turn into saucepan and heat until thickened, stirring as mixture cooks. If you use greens, allow only the 5 minutes needed for thickening. Firmer vegetables may be cooked in the soup up to 10 minutes. Avoid violent boiling. Add butter, 1 or 2 tablespoons, before serving soup.

Soups with Stock, Not Milk

Use the same pattern for soups from meat stock, substituting the stock for milk and cutting down the seasoning if the stock is seasoned. Use 2 bouillon cubes and 2 cups water, or a can of consomme diluted with a can of water if you haven't any meat stock.

Almond Soup

(4 servings)

Rich and aristocratic.

Sauté in a little butter until pale brown

> 1 cup blanched almonds

Turn into the blender container and add

> 1 cup chicken stock or bouillon
> ¼ teaspoon dry mustard
> ¼ teaspoon paprika
> ½ teaspoon sugar
> 1 tablespoon flour

Switch on the motor and blend until almonds have been cut very fine. Turn into saucepan and add

> 2 more cups chicken stock

Heat about 15 minutes and add

> 1 cup cream

Serve as soon as hot. You don't need to sauté the almonds, but if you like a toasty, buttery flavor, I recommend it. Or you can brown half of them in butter and leave the rest plain.

VARIATION: Add a few scraps of ham to the blender mixture.

Cream of Fresh Asparagus Soup

(6 servings)

One of springtime's nicest treats.

Wash and trim away tough parts of stalks of

> 1½ pounds fresh asparagus

Reserve tender tips. Cook stalks in boiling, salted water to cover with

> 1 sliced onion

Purée stalks in blender, keeping cooking water, and adding

> 1½ teaspoons salt
> ⅛ teaspoon pepper
> ⅛ teaspoon nutmeg
> 3 tablespoons butter
> 3 tablespoons flour

Return to saucepot and add

> 3 cups milk

Cook and stir until soup thickens. Serve hot garnished with the tender tips, cooked separately in salted water.

Note: Canned, frozen cooked or leftover asparagus makes wonderful soup together with leftover mashed potatoes and milk—when you have a blender!

Avocado Soup

(4 servings)

Party stuff, and so easy!

Blend until smooth

> 1 large avocado, diced
> 1 cup cream

Heat in saucepan

> 2 cups well-seasoned chicken stock

Add avocado and cream and barely heat through. Garnish with whipped cream. If you have an extra avocado, dice some of it into your soup bowls. You might run whipped-cream-topped bowls of soup under the broiler for a minute if the pottery can take the heat. Half clam broth and half chicken broth turns this into an epicure's dream, especially if you add 2 tablespoons of sherry at the last. And the soup can be served cold, too!

Avocado Yogurt Soup

(4 servings)

Make it an hour or two early—it keeps good color and flavor.

In blender container place

> 1 large or 2 small ripe avocados, peeled, cut in
> pieces
> ½ cup beef, veal or chicken bouillon
> 1 slice onion
> 3 tablespoons lime juice
> 1 teaspoon chili powder
> ½ teaspoon salt

Blend smooth, add

> 1 cup yogurt

Blend a few seconds more, and chill. Buttermilk or light cream with a little sour cream in it may double for yogurt. A delicious first course!

Beet Borsch

(4 servings)

A genuine appetizer.

Place in blender container

> 1 cup pared, diced raw beets
> 1 small onion, quartered
> 1 cup diced potato
> 1 cup chicken or beef stock or bouillon

Blend until vegetables are chopped. Turn into saucepan with

> 1 tablespoon lemon juice
> 1 teaspoon sugar
> Dash of celery salt
> 1 cup more stock
> Salt, pepper to taste

Simmer 10 minutes to blend flavors. Serve cold or hot with sour cream on top.

Borsch in a Hurry

(6 servings)

Tongue-tingling!

Place in blender container and blend until beets are liquefied

> 1 can (1 pound) sliced beets (or 2 cups whole beets,
> cut in quarters)
> 1½ cups tomato juice
> ½ cup water
> Juice of 2 lemons (or 5 tablespoons lemon juice)
> 1-inch strip of lemon peel
> 2 tablespoons sugar
> ½ teaspoon salt

Heat soup to boiling, then cool and refrigerate. At serving time mix in

> ½ cup sour cream

Top portions with

> ½ cup more sour cream

Cream of Broccoli Soup

(6 servings)

Cauliflower soup may be made in the same way.

Place in saucepan

> 1 bunch broccoli, washed and cut into 2-inch pieces
> (discard tough portions of stem)
> ½ cup boiling water
> 1 teaspoon salt

Heat to boiling; cover, reduce heat and steam 30 minutes. Reserve a few broccoli buds to garnish the soup. Purée broccoli, half at a time in blender, with

2 cups chicken broth (use half with each portion of broccoli)

Empty container each time into soup pot.

Stir together over low heat

¼ cup butter
¼ cup flour
1 teaspoon salt

Add gradually

2 cups milk

Cook and stir until smooth and thickened. Add white sauce to broccoli along with

3 chopped green onions, sautéed 5 minutes in
1 tablespoon butter

Heat gently to just under boiling point. Serve soup garnished with reserved broccoli buds.

Buttermilk Watercress Soup

(6 servings)

Keep out a few leaves of cress for garnish.

Place in container of blender

1½ cups buttermilk
1 can cream of celery soup, undiluted
½ teaspoon salt
Dash tabasco sauce
½ cucumber, cut in chunks
1 slice onion or 4 green onions with tops, in 1-inch pieces
1 bunch watercress

Whirl ingredients together until vegetables are fine. Chill for several hours before serving.

Tomato Buttermilk Soup

(4 servings)

Pink and tangy, with a peppery accent.

Place in blender container

> 2 cups buttermilk
> 4 green onions, cut in 1-inch pieces (use tops also)
> ¼ green pepper, in squares, optional
> 1 can condensed tomato soup
> ¼ teaspoon worcestershire sauce
> Few drops tabasco sauce
> ½ teaspoon salt

Blend about 20 seconds. Chill and serve garnished with sprigs of watercress or dabs of sour cream. An excellent first course in summer.

Green Tweed Soup

(8 servings)

A dieter's delight—cold and lovely, but low in calorie count.

Place in blender container

> 1 cup buttermilk
> 1½ teaspoons salt
> ½ green pepper, in squares
> 2 crisp cucumbers, sliced
> ¼ cup packed parsley
> 6 green onions, with tops, cut in 1-inch pieces

Blend until vegetables are chopped fine. Turn into container and add

> 3 cups more buttermilk (remainder of a quart)
> 1 teaspoon worcestershire sauce
> ½ teaspoon celery seeds

Black pepper
¼ teaspoon dill weed

Chill soup and serve garnished with paper-thin slices of un-
pared cucumber.

Lobster Buttermilk Soup

(For 4)

Fresh herbs make all the difference!

Place in blender container

½ cup cooked or canned lobster meat or shrimp
1 small cucumber, diced
½ bunch watercress
1 spray fresh dill, cut in pieces
1 teaspoon prepared mustard
1 teaspoon sugar
2 cups buttermilk

Whirl these ingredients in your blender until everything's in
fine particles, then add

1 cup more buttermilk
Salt to taste

Serve chilly, topped with freshly clipped chives.

Irish Cabbage and Potato Soup

(5 or more servings)

It's hearty, it's good!

Blender-chop separately, then combine in saucepot

¼ head firm cabbage, cut in pieces
1 medium onion, quartered
2 medium pared potatoes, diced

Add

2 cups well-seasoned beef stock, ham stock or
corned beef stock

2 teaspoons salt (amount depends on stock—taste!)
¼ teaspoon black pepper

Cook covered, at simmering, until vegetables are soft. Add

2 cups milk

Heat again, adjust seasonings to taste, and serve in bowls, topping each portion with

½ slice crisp cooked, crumbled bacon
A sprinkle of chopped parsley

Carrot Cream Soup with Cheese

(4 or 5 servings)

Has palate appeal.

Blend until grated, then set aside

½ cup diced hard (natural) cheddar cheese

Place in blender container

2 cups milk
1 slice medium-sized onion
4 medium-sized carrots, cut in chunks
5 sprigs parsley
¼ cup flour
1¼ teaspoons salt
¼ teaspoon pepper

Switch on motor and let it run until carrots are finely chopped but not liquefied. Turn into saucepan and add

2 cups more milk

Cook and stir until thickened. Stir in

3 tablespoons butter
The grated cheese

Serve at once. This soup has a really fresh carrot flavor because of the brief cooking.

Cream of Cauliflower Soup

(6 servings)

The flavor is delicate if the cauliflower is not overcooked.

Cut up and cook until just tender in 4 cups boiling, salted water (keep stock)

>1 head cauliflower

Sauté 2 or 3 minutes

>1 slice onion, in
>¼ cup butter

Purée cauliflower and onion in blender, using some of the stock, and being careful not to fill blender too full. Empty into saucepot. With last batch of cauliflower, add to blender

>¼ cup flour

Blend to mix, turn into saucepot and bring to boiling. Cook until thickened. Add gradually

>2 cups milk
>Salt, pepper, dash of cayenne

Pour a little of the hot soup into

>1 slightly beaten egg

Mix well, then add egg to rest of soup, stirring vigorously. Serve soup very hot. Sprinkle with

>Parmesan cheese

Cherry Soup

(3 servings)

A little spice, and very nice!

>2 cups pitted fresh or canned cherries, sweet or sour, with their juice and ½ cup water

½ cup orange juice
Outer peel of ½ orange
Dash of salt
¼ teaspoon cinnamon
⅓ cup sugar (more for tart cherries)
1 tablespoon cornstarch

Blend until cherries are finely chopped, pour into saucepan and cook and stir until clear-looking. Chill and serve with whipped-cream topping. You'll have to taste and estimate the sugar for yourself. It varies a lot with the kind of cherries used.

Chestnut and Squash Soup

(4 servings)

Decidedly different, and decidedly delicious, too!

Boil for 5 minutes, then remove outer shell and peel of

½ pound chestnuts

Sauté in 2 tablespoons butter

¼ cup diced onion
¼ cup sliced celery
¼ cup sliced carrot

Add chestnuts and the following ingredients

1 bay leaf
1½ cups beef stock
1½ teaspoons sugar

Simmer until chestnuts are soft. Remove bay leaf. Cool somewhat, then place in blender container with

1 cup cooked squash

Blend until ingredients are smooth. Pour back into saucepan and add

½ cup cream

If the soup seems thick, dilute with more stock. Add salt if you need it, and serve garnished with whipped cream and cut chives.

Chili Soup

(6 servings)

Hot or cold, it is hearty and good.

Cook together slowly in a saucepan for 30 minutes, then purée in blender (in several batches)

> 1 can (1 pound) kidney beans
> 1 carrot, sliced
> 1 onion, quartered
> 1 bay leaf (remove after cooking)
> 2 whole cloves (remove after cooking)
> 1½ cups chicken broth
> 1½ cups milk
> ½ teaspoon salt
> 1½ teaspoons chili powder
> 1 long strip outer lemon rind

Chill or heat soup, depending upon how you wish to serve it. Add

> 1 cup cream
> ½ avocado, diced (add just before serving)

Serve hot or cold.

Crabmeat Bisque

(5 or 6 servings)

You've a head start with a can of potato soup.

Thaw soup and place in blender top

> 1 can frozen potato soup
> 1 soup can milk
> 1 can (6¼-7½ ounces) crabmeat

Blend smooth, pour into a saucepan and add

> 1 can (13¾ ounces) chicken broth
> 1 teaspoon salt
> Dash tabasco sauce

Heat and add

> 1 cup cream

Bring just to simmering point and serve sprinkled with chives. A tablespoonful of sherry or Madeira may be poured into each soup cup before you add the hot soup. This bisque also is good served chilled.

Cheese and Crabmeat Soup

(8 servings)

Chunks of seafood in a smooth, delectable cream.

Cook until crisp and set aside

> 4 slices bacon

Sauté in bacon drippings

> 1 cup diced onions

Place bacon and onions in blender container with

> ¼ cup flour
> 1 teaspoon each: salt, pepper, dry mustard, paprika
> 1 bay leaf
> 1 cup milk

Blend until smooth and add gradually

> 2 cups diced cheddar cheese
> 1 cup bouillon, or veal or chicken broth

Blend until smooth again. Turn into saucepan and add

> 2 cups more milk

Cook over moderate heat and stir until soup thickens. Add

1 can (6½-7¼ ounces) crabmeat, in chunks

Heat through and serve.

Cold Cranberry Soup

(4 servings)

Colorful, tart and delicious.
Cook together for 10 minutes

2 cups fresh cranberries
1 cup sugar
1 tablespoon tapioca
¼ stick cinnamon
2 slices lemon
2 cups water

Remove cinnamon and 1 lemon slice. Purée rest of mixture in blender. Chill and serve garnished with whipped cream.

Cold Cucumber Soup

(6 servings)

A delectable relative of vichyssoise.
In large skillet place

2 tablespoons butter
1 onion, sliced
2 green onions with stems, cut in pieces

Cook gently for 5 minutes. Add

4 chicken bouillon cubes
3 cups hot water
½ cup packed parsley stems and leaves
2 or 3 pieces celery about 6 inches long, cut in pieces
3 medium potatoes, pared, quartered
½ teaspoon thyme

Cover and cook on low heat until potatoes are tender. Place ingredients in blender (in several batches) and whirl fine. Chill. Add and chill for several hours, covered

> Dash tabasco sauce
> 2 cups sour cream
> 1 teaspoon salt
> 1 medium cucumber, chopped fine (may be blender-chopped)

Serve in cold bowls garnished with thin slices of cucumber, peel on.

Curry Soup

(4 servings)

For particular people.

Cook together gently for 10 minutes

> ¼ cup butter
> 1 large, sliced sweet onion

Cool somewhat, then transfer to blender and add

> 2½ cups beef, veal or chicken stock or bouillon
> 1 teaspoon curry powder
> ¼ teaspoon ginger
> ¼ teaspoon nutmeg
> 2 tablespoons flour
> 1 egg

Blend smooth, turn into saucepan and cook gently until thick and smooth. Add

> 1 cup cream
> 2 tablespoons sherry

Heat gently, but do not boil.

Gazpacho

(6 to 8 servings)

Here's that famous Spanish soup in a delicious version.

In blender container place

> 1 cup tomato juice
> ¼ cup olive oil
> 1 clove garlic

Blend until garlic is fine. Add and blend until chopped coarse

> 2 medium tomatoes, skinned, quartered
> 1 medium onion, cut in chunks
> 1 green pepper, in pieces

Add,* but do not blend further

> 1 can condensed consommé
> 3 tablespoons wine vinegar
> Salt, pepper as necessary

Serve in chilled bowls with an ice cube in each serving. Whipped cream or sour cream may be used as garnish, but isn't necessary.

* If your blender holds only a quart, empty into another container.

Green Pepper Meat Soup

(6 servings)

Substantial lunch.

Place in blender container

> 2 large green peppers, cut in pieces
> 1 large onion, diced

2 cups canned tomatoes
2 slices half-cooked bacon, diced

Blend until ingredients are chopped, but not too fine. Place in saucepan with

1 quart meat stock or consommé
1 pound hamburger
Salt and pepper as needed

Cover pan and bring to boil; reduce heat and simmer for 1 hour.

Ham and Lima Bean Soup

(6 servings)

The hammier the ham, the better the soup!

Simmer together for 3 or 4 hours, or until beans are soft, in 8 cups water

1 meaty ham hock
1 cup large dry lima beans
1 onion
1 clove garlic
1 bay leaf

Remove and discard bone. Clip ham cross-grain with scissors, and reserve. Purée beans and stock in blender, 2 cups or so at a time. Return to soup kettle with ham, season to taste with salt and pepper, and heat just to the simmering point. Good with crisp chunky bread.

Lentil Soup

(4 to 6 servings)

Garnish with sliced sausage, sour cream and chives.

Simmer together for 2 hours or longer, in covered soup pot

1 cup lentils
1 quart chicken broth, ham stock or bouillon

　　　1 teaspoon salt
　　　1 bay leaf
　　　1 clove garlic
　　　1 small onion
　　　A few celery leaves

Purée in blender, 2 cups or so at a time. (Remove bay leaf.)
Return to soup pot and add more liquid if needed, plus

　　　1 can Vienna sausages, sliced

Adjust seasonings, ladle into soup bowls and garnish with
sour cream and chopped chives.

Cream of Lettuce Soup

(6 servings)

*Delicately flavored; top it with sour cream and shredded raw
carrot.*

Heat to boiling, then simmer for 15 minutes and purée in
blender

　　　2 cups shredded lettuce
　　　½ cup celery leaves
　　　1 small onion, in pieces
　　　1 green pepper, diced
　　　2½ cups water
　　　1½ teaspoons salt

Mix together

　　　2 egg yolks
　　　2 cups milk
　　　2 cups light cream or evaporated milk

Add puréed vegetables and

　　　¼ cup butter, optional

Heat just to boiling point, and serve immediately.

Mushroom Cream Soup

(3 servings)

The richest, but surely the best, you've ever eaten!

Cook together for 5 minutes

> ½ pound washed, dried mushrooms (*fresh* ones)
> ¼ pound (1 stick) butter

Cool and turn into the blender container with

> 2 cups chicken stock

Blend until mushrooms are coarsely chopped and add

> 3 egg yolks

Blend just a second or two and turn into a saucepan with 1 cup cream. Stir and heat gently until thickened. Season, if necessary, with salt and pepper.

Olive Soup

(6 servings)

This unusual soup has a piquancy you'll enjoy.

Cook together gently for 5 minutes

> 3 tablespoons butter
> 1 onion, quartered
> 6 ribs celery, in ½-inch pieces

Cool and turn into blender container with

> ½ cup pimiento-stuffed olives
> ½ cup flour
> 1½ cups water
> 2 teaspoons salt
> ½ teaspoon pepper

Blend until vegetables are chopped fairly fine. Turn into saucepan and add

½ cup water
2 cups milk

Cook over low heat until smooth and thickened. If the soup seems thick, add a little more water or milk.

Queen of Onion Soups

(6 servings)

On a blustery night, the perfect warmer!

Place in large skillet

> 4 large onions, sliced thick
> 3 tablespoons butter

Cook gently for 5 minutes and add

> 4 cups beef stock or bouillon
> 1 teaspoon salt
> ½ teaspoon pepper
> 1½ cups sliced potatoes

Cover skillet and cook until potatoes are tender. Purée in blender, about 2 cups at a time, and empty into saucepot. Taste and add more seasonings, if necessary. Heat and add

> 1 cup cream

Heat again but do not allow to boil. Place in each of 6 soup bowls a slice of toasted French bread. Pour soup into bowls and sprinkle with

> ½ cup grated sharp cheese

Oyster Bisque

(6 servings)

A creamy-textured beginning for a holiday dinner.

Heat together in a saucepan just to boiling point

> 1 pint oysters, picked over (keep liquid)
> 2 sprigs parsley

> 2 clusters celery tips and leaves
> 1 slice onion
> Piece of bay leaf
> 1 cup milk
> ⅓ cup flour

Remove bay leaf and purée everything in blender. Return to saucepan and add

> 3 cups more milk (4 cups for thinner soup)
> ¼ cup butter
> Salt, pepper to taste

Heat and stir until soup thickens. Keep warm over low heat or in top of double boiler for 10 to 15 minutes to develop full flavor. Serve with toast sticks or fried croutons.

Tomato Oyster Bisque

(6 servings)

An "R" season favorite.

Pick over and remove any bits of shell from

> 1 pint oysters

Place in blender container with oyster liquor and

> 1 cup milk

Blend until oysters are chopped fine. Pour into another container. Into blender place

> 1 slice onion
> 1 tablespoon flour
> 2 teaspoons salt
> ¼ teaspoon pepper
> 1 can condensed tomato soup
> 2 cups milk

Blend a few seconds, turn into saucepan and cook, stirring constantly until thickened. Add oysters and

1 cup cream
2 tablespoons butter

Serve as soon as hot.

Cream of Parsley Soup

(4 servings)

Green as the sod of Ireland!

Mince fine in blender

> 1 cup packed parsley, coarse stalks removed
> (about ½ bunch)
> 2 cups chicken, veal or beef stock or bouillon

Simmer for 30 minutes in a saucepan. Meanwhile mix in another saucepan

> 3 tablespoons melted butter
> 3 tablespoons flour
> 1 teaspoon salt
> ¼ teaspoon pepper

Heat together, stirring constantly. Add gradually

> 2 cups milk

Cook and stir until sauce thickens. Add the parsley and broth, also

> ½ cup cream

Heat well but do not allow to boil. Serve garnished with whipped cream or sour cream, if you wish.

Fresh Pea Soup

(4 servings)

You might serve it cold with a garnish of chopped mint, for a sometime variation.

Cook together until vegetables are tender

> 1 cup fresh peas or ½ package frozen
> 2 ribs celery with leaves, cross-cut in pieces
> ½ small head lettuce, in chunks
> 1 slice onion
> 3 chicken bouillon cubes in
> 2 cups water
> 1 teaspoon salt
> ¼ teaspoon pepper
> A pinch of rosemary

Purée in blender and return to saucepan. Heat and add

> 1 cup more peas or the other ½ package frozen peas

Cook 5 to 8 minutes, until peas are tender. Stir into soup

> 1 cup heavy cream

Heat through and serve.

Note: The tiny peas in butter sauce from the frozen foods department make a delicious soup. Use the butter sauce, and finish with light cream instead of heavy cream.

Yellow Pea Soup

(A Czechoslovakian recipe; 4 or more servings)

Easy to make and full of flavor.

Cook together at simmering for 2 hours, then purée in blender

> 1 pound dried yellow peas (about 2 cups)
> 2 quarts water
> 1 teaspoon salt

Sauté

> 1 small onion, sliced
> 1 clove garlic in
> ¼ cup butter

Purée in blender with a little of the soup. Combine with rest of pea soup mixture and add

>1 teaspoon salt (more, if needed)
>1 teaspoon marjoram
>¼ teaspoon pepper

Heat to the boiling point. Serve topped with garlic croutons and minced parsley.

Pimiento Cream Soup

(6 servings)

Pretty color; interesting flavor.

Place in blender container

>¼ cup parsley
>4 pimientos and juice
>1 slice onion
>3 tablespoons flour
>2 cups milk
>1 egg

Blend these ingredients until parsley is finely chopped, and pour into saucepan with

>3 cups more milk
>¼ cup chili sauce
>1 teaspoon salt

Cook and stir until thickened and serve topped with paprika.

Cream of Potato Soup

(6 servings)

One of my family's favorite soups.

Cook together until potatoes are tender

>4 cups sliced potatoes (about 4 medium)

>   2 cups water
>   2 teaspoons salt

Sauté

>   1 small sliced onion, in
>   3 tablespoons butter

Place potatoes, cooking water, and onion in blender container and blend smooth with

>   4 or 5 sprigs parsley
>   2 tablespoons flour

Return to saucepot and add

>   3 cups milk

Stir and heat to simmering. Season to taste with

>   Salt, black pepper

POTATO CHEESE SOUP: Stir in 1½ cups grated sharp cheese shortly before serving.

If soup is thicker than you like it, thin with milk or cream.

POTATO WATERCRESS SOUP: Substitute about ¼ bunch watercress for the parsley.

Locro (Ecuadorean Potato Soup)

(6 to 8 servings)

Utterly delicious; a conversation piece.

Chop fine in blender

>   3 medium onions

Sauté them in

>   ¼ cup butter, along with
>   2 cloves
>   2 bay leaves
>   2 teaspoons salt

8 peppercorns
⅛ teaspoon saffron (or 1 teaspoon crushed annatto
    seeds)

Add

2 quarts (8 cups) water
3 pounds (about 8 medium) potatoes, diced

Cook 30 to 40 minutes, until potatoes are tender. Add

½ pound Gruyère cheese, grated in blender with
1 cup milk or cream
1 egg

Simmer gently until soup is thickened and smooth. Serve with mixed green salad including ripe tomatoes, and crusty bread.

Scandinavian Fruit Soup

(6 or more servings)

This one can precede or follow the entree.

Cook together until tender

½ pound dried prunes, pitted
½ pound dried apricots
3 apples, cored and diced
½ cup sugar
1½ quarts water or fruit juice and water
1 stick cinnamon

Remove cinnamon and purée the fruits in your blender (not all at once). Return fruits to saucepan and add

2 tablespoons cornstarch mixed with a little cold
    water

Cook and stir until clear-looking. Chill and serve very cold. Can be flavored with port wine—about a tablespoonful per serving.

Cold Spanish Soup

(6 servings)

Garlicky, but very good, and pretty, too.

Tear into pieces and grate in blender to fine crumbs

> 2 slices bread, crusts removed

Empty into bowl. In blender container place

> ¼ cup chicken broth or bouillon (from 1 can, or 2 cups total)
> 3 cloves garlic
> 10 toasted almonds
> 1 teaspoon salt
> Dash pepper
> 2 tablespoons olive oil

Blend until garlic and nuts are very fine. Mix with crumbs. An hour before you wish to serve the soup, add

> Remainder of broth or bouillon (about 1¾ cups)
> 8 ice cubes

Just before serving add

> ½ tablespoon vinegar
> 2 cups chopped cantaloupe (hand chop, not too fine)

Serve in chilled bowls as a first course.

Sao Paulo Spinach Soup

(6 servings)

From Brazil, but not alien to North American palates!

In blender container place

> 2 cups cooked spinach or 2 (10-ounce) packages frozen chopped spinach, thawed
> ¼ cup (½ stick) butter

2 teaspoons brown sugar
¼ teaspoon nutmeg
¼ teaspoon garlic salt
1 cup chicken or veal stock

Blend until spinach is fine. Place in saucepan and add

2 cups more chicken or veal stock

Simmer 10 minutes, then add

1 cup heavy cream

Heat through and serve with garnish of a little more whipped cream, if you wish.

Fresh Tomato Cream Soup

(4 servings)

No curdle; fresh flavor.

Place in blender container

2 cups milk
½ teaspoon salt
1 tablespoon flour

Blend a few seconds, then cook in saucepan until thickened, stirring constantly. Meanwhile, put into blender container

4 medium-sized ripe tomatoes, coarse-diced
3 sprigs parsley
1 teaspoon sugar
Sprinkle of cloves
2 slices onion
½ teaspoon salt
¼ teaspoon pepper

Whirl until smooth and add tomato purée gradually to hot white sauce, stirring constantly. Serve as soon as thoroughly hot, with sour cream or whipped cream on top. Be sure to taste the soup for seasonings. You may need a little more salt.

Vichyssoise

(4 servings)

Cold elegance.

Cook together gently for 5 minutes

> 4 big leeks, sliced (use tops, too)
> 3 tablespoons butter

Turn into blender with

> 3 medium-sized potatoes, diced
> 2 cups chicken broth

Blend until vegetables are very fine. Pour into saucepan and add

> 1 cup more chicken broth
> Salt, white pepper as needed

Cook gently 10 minutes and add

> ¾ cup heavy cream

Chill and serve with cut chives on each portion.

Watercress Soup

(For 4 gourmets)

Full of vitamins, too.

Place in blender container

> 1 bunch washed watercress
> 1 tablespoon flour
> 2 cups chicken broth, bouillon or consommé

Blend until cress is finely chopped, turn into saucepan and heat through with

> 1 cup cream

Garnish with whipped cream, sprinkle with paprika.

12 | Vegetables

At first thought you might dismiss the electric blender as far as vegetables are concerned. But for soufflés and vegetable rings, the blender can reduce a raw or cooked vegetable to the required fine particles. The blender can also prepare the fine crumbs to top a vegetable casserole, the grated cheese for au gratin dishes. It can mince the onion, garlic and green pepper needed to season some vegetable combinations, and help prepare the smooth white-sauce base for others.

Blender-chopped nuts, plain or toasted, dress up a green vegetable such as asparagus or broccoli beautifully. After chopping the nuts you can sauté them in a little butter for added "toothsomeness." Cooked chestnuts can be chopped in a blender to dress another vegetable (Brussels sprouts, for example) or puréed entirely if you like them puréed.

Stuffed Artichokes

(4 servings)

If you love artichokes you'll call these divine!

Parboil in salted water for 10 minutes

4 fresh artichokes, trimmed,* chokes removed

* Cut off stems so that artichokes will sit up prettily, cut off top third of leaves and trim off any brown outer ones.

Mince in blender

> ¼ cup diced ham
> 6 fresh mushrooms
> 4 green onions with tops, cut in 1-inch slices
> 4 sprigs parsley
> 2 tablespoons mayonnaise

With the filling thus prepared, stuff hearts of artichokes and spread filling between the leaves. Place in baking dish with

> ½ cup white wine
> ½ cup well-seasoned chicken broth
> 1 garlic clove
> 1 sprig parsley
> Sprinkle of chopped fresh or frozen chives

Sprinkle artichokes with

> 2 tablespoons olive oil

Cover and bake 40 minutes at 350°.

Asparagus Casserole

(4 servings)

A pleasing luncheon entree.

Prepare in blender

> 1 cup soft bread crumbs (2 slices bread)

Place half the crumbs in greased baking dish. Place alternate layers of the following in baking dish

> 1 pound asparagus, cut in 1-inch pieces, cooked
> 4 hard-cooked eggs, sliced
> 2 pimientos, cut in strips

In blender container place

> 2 tablespoons butter
> 2 tablespoons flour
> ½ teaspoon salt

1 cup milk
1 cup cheddar cheese, diced

Blend smooth and pour over asparagus and eggs. Top with remainder of crumbs. Dot with

2 tablespoons butter

Bake in moderate oven, 350°, for 30 minutes.

Asparagus-Nut Scallop

(4 servings)

The method is a good one for other vegetables.

Convert to fine crumbs in the blender and set aside

1 slice buttered toast, broken into pieces

Blender-chop, not too fine

½ cup peanuts, toasted almonds or pecans

Place in buttered shallow baking dish

2 cups cooked or canned drained asparagus cuts

Sprinkle with the chopped nuts and cover with

1½ cups well-seasoned medium white sauce, page 275

Sprinkle with the reserved crumbs and bake at 400° for 20 minutes.

Green Beans in Olive Cream Sauce

(Six servings)

Makes those beans important!

Blender-grate and set aside

1 slice buttered toast, broken in pieces
½ cup diced sharp cheddar cheese

Prepare

> 2 cups medium white sauce, page 275, adding and chopping
> ¼ cup stuffed olives

Pour sauce over

> 1 pound cooked green beans

Top with reserved crumbs, cheese and

> 2 slices crisp, crumbled bacon

Bake 30 minutes at 350°.
Canned or frozen cooked green beans may be used, of course.

Kidney Bean Casserole

(6 servings)

A perfect pot luck, picnic or buffet dish.

Blender-chop, a few slices at a time, not too fine

> 3 apples, cored and sliced
> 2 medium onions

Mix in casserole with

> 2 cups drained cooked or canned kidney beans
> ¼ cup brown sugar
> ½ pound pre-cooked pork sausage, drained of fat, crumbled
> 1 can (8 ounces) tomato sauce
> 1½ teaspoons salt
> ¼ teaspoon pepper

Bake uncovered at 350° for 1 hour.

Burgundy Beans

(6 servings)

Perfect for a winter buffet.

Simmer for an hour

> 2 cups kidney or pink beans
> 1 slice salt pork
> 1 quart water

Place ingredients in a casserole. Place in the blender container

> 1 large onion, quartered
> 1 clove garlic
> 1¼ teaspoons salt
> 1 8-ounce can tomato sauce
> 1 tablespoon brown sugar
> 1 teaspoon dry mustard
> ¼ cup salad oil
> ½ teaspoon black pepper

Blend until onion is fine and pour over beans. Mix in

> ½ pound American cheese, cubed

Cover and bake at 275° for 4 hours, adding in small amounts from time to time

> 1 cup Burgundy wine

Casserole of Baked Beans

(6 servings)

Piquantly seasoned and ever so good.

Blender-chop separately

> 1 cup celery, in 1-inch pieces
> ¼ cup stuffed olives
> 2 large sweet pickles, cut in chunks

Add, in baking dish, to

>2 cans (1 pound each) pork and beans
>½ pound sharp cheddar cheese, diced
>½ teaspoon dry mustard
>½ cup catsup
>½ cup brown sugar

Mix well and bake at 350° for 1½ hours.

Rum Baked Beans

(6 servings)

Make it sherry, if you don't care for rum. Exotic!

Simmer 2 hours in water to cover

>1 pound navy beans
>1 ham bone

Drain beans and place in beanpot. Into the blender container put

>1 cup bean liquid
>½ cup brown sugar
>2 onions, quartered
>1 sliver garlic
>1½ teaspoons salt
>½ bay leaf
>¼ teaspoon pepper

Blend until onions are finely chopped. Pour over beans. Add more bean liquid to cover. Cover and bake at 275° about 4 hours. Add the last half hour

>½ cup rum (or sherry)

I sometimes add a small can of crushed pineapple to these beans.

Tasty Beans

(4 servings)

New England would never know them!

Crumb in blender and set aside

> 1 slice buttered toast, broken in pieces

Blender-chop, ½ cup at a time

> 2 small onions, quartered or diced
> 2 green peppers, cut in squares

Sauté the vegetables for 5 minutes in

> 2 tablespoons butter

Season with salt and pepper and place in layers in buttered dish with

> 1 pound can baked beans
> ¾ cup grated sharp cheese (blender-grated or from a can)

Top with reserved crumbs and bake at 375° for 30 minutes.

Beets with Sour Cream Sauce

(6 servings)

Drained canned beets may be prepared in this way, too, of course.

Boil until tender, slip off skins, quarter and blender-chop

> 2 bunches fresh beets

In skillet melt

> 2 tablespoons butter

Stir in

> 1 tablespoon flour
> 3 tablespoons vinegar
> 2 tablespoons sugar

Add chopped beets, heat gently, stir to blend flavors and add

> Salt and pepper to taste

When thoroughly hot, add

> ½ cup sour cream

Stir and serve promptly.

Piquant Beets

(6 servings)

Beets in a hurry, this dish!

> 3 cups pared sliced raw beets
> ¾ cup water
> ¼ cup vinegar (tarragon, if you have it)
> 2 tablespoons butter
> 1 teaspoon salt
> ⅛ teaspoon pepper
> ½ cup sugar
> 2 tablespoons cornstarch

Blend until beets are chopped coarsely. Turn into saucepan and cook and stir over moderate heat about 15 minutes, until thickened and cooked throughout. You can use lemon juice in place of vinegar and add a strip of lemon peel to the ingredients if you'd rather.

Broccoli Loaf

(6 servings)

A main course this way.

Chop in blender cooked broccoli to make

>2 cups chopped broccoli

Turn into pan. Into blender place

>2 eggs
>1 cup canned tomatoes
>1 slice medium-sized onion
>1 cup diced celery
>3 tablespoons butter
>½ teaspoon salt
>¼ teaspoon pepper

Blend to chop vegetables. Add to broccoli with

>1 cup coarse cracker crumbs

Bake in greased loaf pan at 350°, moderate oven, about 40 minutes. Serve with White Sauce (page 275) or cheese sauce.

Quick Creamy Cabbage

(4 servings)

As good as it is easy!

Blender-chop

>½ medium head cabbage, cut into chunks

Add ½ cup water and cook 5 minutes, covered. Sprinkle cabbage with

>2 tablespoons flour

Add and stir until sauce thickens

>1 cup milk or cream
>1 teaspoon salt (more if needed)
>⅛ teaspoon pepper

Cabbage should be slightly crisp. A pinch of curry seasoning might be added, if you like curry.

Sweet-Sour Cabbage

(6 servings)

Use this recipe with red cabbage as well as green.

Blender-chop

>2 apples, pared, cored, sliced
>1 onion, cut in quarters

Sauté for 5 minutes in

>2 tablespoons bacon, ham or sausage drippings, or butter

Blender-chop, in small amounts, emptying into skillet with apples and onion

>½ head cabbage, cut into chunks

Add

>½ cup water (water may be used to aid in chopping, if you wish)

Cover and cook gently 20 minutes. Then add

>⅓ cup brown sugar
>½ cup vinegar
>Salt, pepper to taste

Stir together well and serve hot.

Bohemian Sauerkraut

(6 or more servings)

This is a European favorite. Some nationalities like more apple, and add brown sugar.

Blender-chop

>1 onion, quartered

Sauté for 5 minutes in

>   2 tablespoons butter

Add

>   1 small potato, diced and chopped in blender
>   1 apple, pared, cored, sliced and chopped in blender
>   3 cups sauerkraut
>   1 teaspoon or more caraway seeds

Simmer together until flavors blend, about 20 minutes, and serve with frankfurters. Or place in pan with spareribs, pork loin or other meat.

Red Cabbage with Currant Jelly

(4 servings)

Sweet, tart and fruity, a most delicious vegetable.

Blender-chop

>   Red cabbage, cut in chunks, to make 4 cups
>   2 tart cooking apples, pared, cored, sliced
>   1 small onion, quartered

Combine in saucepan and add

>   2½ tablespoons butter
>   1 tablespoon vinegar

Cover tight and steam 5 to 8 minutes. Add

>   2 tablespoons currant jelly
>   ½ teaspoon salt (or more)
>   ¼ teaspoon pepper

Heat through and serve.

Carrot and Peanut Bake

(5 servings)

A good school-day luncheon.

Blender-chop fine, and place in 2-quart casserole

>Carrots to make 1¼ cups
>1 small onion, quartered
>1¼ cups salted peanuts

Add

>1¼ cups canned or fresh tomatoes
>1 teaspoon salt
>¼ teaspoon pepper
>2 egg yolks, beaten lightly

Fold in

>2 egg whites, beaten stiff

Set casserole in a pan of warm water and bake at 350° for 1 hour. Serve with parsley cream sauce made by adding 2 tablespoons or more chopped parsley to 1½ cups medium white sauce, page 275. Parsley can be chopped in the sauce. Use 6 or 8 sprigs.

Carrot Ring

(4 servings)

Rule for getting Johnny to eat carrots.

Tear into blender container and cut to crumbs

>1 slice bread

Set aside. Place in container

>3 eggs
>1 slice onion
>4 sprigs parsley
>1 tablespoon melted butter
>1 teaspoon salt
>¼ teaspoon pepper
>2½ cups cooked diced carrots
>1 tablespoon maple sirup or brown sugar

Blend until carrots are finely cut. Fold in bread crumbs and turn into a buttered 8-inch ring mold. Set in a shallow pan of water and bake in moderately hot oven, 375°, for 30 minutes or until firm. Unmold on serving plate and fill with creamed peas. You can use raw carrots, blender-chopping them on low speed, first.

Panned Carrots

(4 or more servings)

An unusual and delicious way to serve a common vegetable.

Blender-chop

> Sliced carrots to make 4 cups
> ¼ green pepper, cut in pieces
> ½ small onion
> 3 or 4 sprigs parsley

Place in heavy saucepan with

> 3 tablespoons butter or oil
> Salt, pepper to taste
> ½ teaspoon sugar

Cover and cook gently until tender, with occasional stirring. Remove cover and allow to brown lightly.

Cauliflower Cottage Cheese Puff

(4 servings)

Much tastier than you'd think!

Crumb in blender and set aside

> 2 slices buttered bread, broken apart

Blender-chop and add to crumbs

> Cooked cauliflower, sliced, to make 1½ cups

In blender container place

> 2 egg yolks
> 1 cup cottage cheese
> 1 slice onion
> ¾ teaspoon salt
> ¼ teaspoon pepper

Blend smooth and mix with cauliflower and crumbs. Fold in

> 2 egg whites, beaten stiff

Turn into greased 1-quart casserole, set in a pan of hot water and bake at 350° for 40 minutes, or until firm.

BROCCOLI COTTAGE CHEESE PUFF: Same, but with broccoli.

Cauliflower with Crumbs and Nuts

(4 servings)

A quickie with flavor.

Cook until tender, whole or broken apart

> 1 medium-sized head cauliflower

Break into blender container and cut into fine crumbs

> 1 slice bread

Empty crumbs into saucepan with

> ¼ cup melted butter

Add

> ¼ cup nuts (pecans, preferably), ground fine in blender

Brown lightly over moderate heat and pour over the salted and peppered cauliflower.

Corn and Tomato Casserole

(6 servings)

A delicious combination to which you could add some cheese.

Blender-chop

> 1 small onion, quartered
> 1 green pepper, cut in pieces

Sauté onion and pepper for 5 minutes in

> 2 tablespoons butter

Drain

> 1 can whole-kernel corn (or use 2 cups cut from cob)

Slice thick

> 4 to 6 tomatoes

Place half the corn in a buttered casserole, cover with half the tomatoes, onion and green pepper, and sprinkle with

> 1 teaspoon salt
> ¼ teaspoon pepper

Repeat the procedure. Cover with

> 3 slices diced bacon
> 1 cup blender-prepared soft crumbs

Bake at 375° for 30 minutes.

Corn Pie

(A 9-incher; for 5)

With salad, a good lunch.

Line a 9-inch pie pan with

> Plain pie pastry (½ recipe or ½ package mix)

Build rim up high. Place in blender container

 1 cup light cream
 1 teaspoon salt
 1 slice green pepper
 1 slice onion
 5 sprigs parsley
 1 egg

Blend about 20 seconds. Add contents of

 1 No. 2 can cream-style corn

Turn into pastry-lined pie pan. Top with

 ½ cup buttered crumbs (crumbs can be made in blender with 1 slice bread)
 ⅓ cup grated cheese

Bake pie in hot oven, 450°, for 10 minutes, then lower heat to 350° for 25 minutes longer or until firm in center.

Nut Stuffed Eggplant

(4 to 6 servings)

So easy to do!

Cook 15 minutes in boiling water

 1 whole eggplant

Drain, cut in half lengthwise and cut out pulp with a spoon, leaving a shell about ¾ inch thick. Place in blender container

 The scooped out eggplant pulp
 4 or 5 sprigs parsley
 ¼ medium-sized onion
 1 egg
 Salt, pepper, dash of marjoram

Switch on motor and let run until ingredients are finely chopped. Mix with

 ½ cup chopped nuts (can be blender-chopped, you know)

2 cups soft bread crumbs (4 slices bread broken into blender, 1 at a time)

Add more salt if you need it and fill eggplant shells. Bake in moderately hot oven, 375°, about 40 minutes, basting occasionally with mixture of

¼ cup water
2 tablespoons butter

Mushroom Soufflé

(6 servings)

If you love mushrooms, you'll cherish this recipe!

Blender-chop, in small portions

1 pound fresh mushrooms, washed in salt water, dried

In blender container place

1 cup cream
½ cup flour
¼ cup soft butter
1½ teaspoons salt
⅛ teaspoon pepper
4 or 5 sprigs parsley

Blend smooth, then turn into saucepan and cook and stir until thickened and smooth. Turn off heat and stir in vigorously

4 egg yolks, slightly beaten

Add the mushrooms and fold in

4 egg whites, beaten stiff

Turn into greased 1½-quart casserole, set in a pan of warm water and bake at 350° for an hour.

Onion Ring

(6 servings)

So good!

Purée in blender enough half-boiled onions to make

>   1 cup onion purée

Add

>   2 tablespoons butter
>   2 tablespoons flour
>   ½ cup milk
>   1 teaspoon salt
>   ⅛ teaspoon pepper
>   ½ cup diced cheese
>   3 egg yolks

Blend a few seconds and pour into saucepan. Cook over moderate heat, stirring constantly until thickened. Remove from heat and fold in

>   3 egg whites, beaten stiff

Pour into buttered ring mold, set in a pan of hot water and bake in a 350° oven about an hour, or until set. A few sprigs of parsley can be added. Turn the ring onto a hot platter and fill center with buttered peas or another bright-colored vegetable.

Potato, Onion and Cheese Bake

(6 servings)

A savory dish to go with the baked ham.

Blender-chop, in small portions, separately

>   4 large potatoes, pared, diced
>   3 medium onions, quartered

Layer the potatoes and onions in buttered baking dish with

> 1 teaspoon salt
> ¼ teaspoon pepper

Pour over the combination

> 1½ cups scalded cream

Sprinkle with

> 4 cups shredded sharp cheddar cheese

Cover casserole and bake at 375° for 35 minutes. Remove cover and bake 10 minutes more.

Peeket (Potato Casserole)

(8 servings)

Starts out like potato pancakes but turns into something different!

Blender-grate in cold water, then drain

> 6 cups cubed potatoes (about 6 medium)

Place in blender container and blend to chop parsley fine

> 3 eggs
> 1¼ teaspoons salt
> ¼ teaspoon pepper
> 1 onion slice
> 5 or 6 sprigs parsley
> 2 tablespoons flour mixed with
> 1 teaspoon baking powder
> ¼ cup milk

Mix with potatoes. Grease 2-quart baking dish and line with

> 6 strips bacon, cut in half

Pour in potato mixture and top with

> 6 more strips bacon, cut in half

Bake 1 hour at 350°.

Potato Puff

(4 servings)

A new way for potatoes.

> 4 sizable potatoes, cut in large dice
> ¼ cup firmly packed parsley
> 1 onion, cut in dice
> ½ green pepper, cut in dice
> 1 cup milk
> 3 eggs
> 1½ teaspoons salt
> ¼ teaspoon pepper
> 1 cup diced cheese
> ½ cup butter

Blend all ingredients until potatoes are finely grated and turn into buttered casserole. Bake in 350° oven for about an hour. If this seems too big a load for your blender, blend 2 cut potatoes and ½ cup milk first, turn into casserole, blend other ingredients and mix.

Potato Roast with Walnuts

(6 servings)

Surprisingly flavorsome.

Chop fine in blender and combine in greased loaf pan

> 1 slice bread, torn in pieces
> 2½ pounds (6 large) potatoes, pared, cut up
> 1 large onion, cut in pieces
> 1 cup walnuts

Add and mix well

> 2 eggs, beaten
> 3 tablespoons melted fat
> ½ teaspoon salt

¼ teaspoon pepper
½ teaspoon powdered sage

Top with, if you wish,

4 bacon strips

Bake at 350° 45 minutes or until firm.

Curried Rice Ring

(12 servings)

To hold creamed chicken, turkey or shrimps.

Place in blender container

4 eggs
2 cups milk
6 tablespoons soft butter
½ cup packed parsley
1 teaspoon curry powder
¼ teaspoon celery seed
1 teaspoon salt
⅛ teaspoon pepper

Blend until parsley is finely cut and pour over

6 cups cooked rice seasoned with salt (1½ cups before cooking)

Stir until well mixed. Fill large greased ring mold. Set mold in a pan of hot water and bake in a moderate oven at 350° for about an hour. Cool for 5 minutes, then turn out on a hot serving platter and fill center of ring with creamed chicken, turkey or fish. This is a good buffet-supper combination. Season the chicken (or turkey) or fish sauce with a little sherry.

Orange Rice

(6 servings)

This is wonderful with a baked ham or roast duck dinner.

Blender-chop

> 1 small onion, quartered
> 1 rib celery with leaves, cut in 1-inch lengths

Sauté in

> 3 tablespoons butter

In blender container place

> Outer peel 1 orange
> 1 cup orange juice

Blend until peel is very fine. Add to sautéed vegetables with

> 1½ cups water
> 1¼ teaspoons salt

Bring to boil and add

> 1 cup rice (not quick-cooking)

Cover, reduce heat and simmer until rice is tender, about 25 minutes.

Spinach or Carrot Soufflé

(5 servings)

Use this recipe for any vegetable soufflé.

Place in blender container

> ¾ cup milk
> ¼ cup soft butter
> 4 egg yolks
> ¼ cup flour
> 1 slice onion
> 1 teaspoon salt
> ⅛ teaspoon pepper
> ½ cup diced cheese
> 2 cups packed, washed raw spinach or 1½ cups diced raw carrot

Blend until vegetable is finely cut. Turn into saucepan and cook and stir until thickened over moderate heat. Cool slightly and fold in

> 4 egg whites, beaten stiff

Turn into greased casserole, sprinkle with paprika and bake in 325° oven 50 minutes to an hour. Serve immediately, by itself or with a tomato or mushroom sauce.

Sweet Potatoes with Bananas

(4 servings)

Tropical treat.

Chop together in blender

> ⅓ cup toasted almonds
> ⅓ cup toasted walnuts

Turn into a bowl with

> 2 cups mashed sweet potatoes (can be blender-mashed)
> 1 tablespoon sugar
> Pinch of salt
> 1 tablespoon butter
> ½ teaspoon vanilla

Crumb in blender

> 1 slice bread

Add to potatoes. Mash in blender

> 2 bananas

Mix with potato combination. Shape into small mounds in well-greased pan. Top each mound with

> Walnut half

Bake in a moderate oven, 350°, for 15 minutes.

Orange Baked Yams

(4 servings)

Lots of flavor here.

Place in baking dish

> 1 can sweet potatoes, sirup-packed, drained of sirup
> and sliced
> 2 tablespoons butter

Place in blender container

> Sirup from potatoes
> Pinch of ginger
> Pinch of mace
> ¼ orange, including peel (no seeds), cut in several
> pieces
> ¼ teaspoon salt
> 1 tablespoon brown sugar

Blend until orange is fine. Pour over potatoes and bake at 350°, moderate oven, 1 hour, basting several times with sirup in dish.

Squash with Orange and Pecans

(4 servings)

If you wish, pile the mixture into orange half-shells, brush with butter and brown at 400°.

In blender container place

> ½ cup orange juice
> Pared outer rind of 1 orange

Blend until peel is fine. Whip until light with

> 2 cups cooked and mashed Hubbard or other winter
> squash
> 1 tablespoon brown sugar

½ teaspoon salt
Dash pepper
2 tablespoons butter
¼ cup blender-chopped pecans

Pile in casserole dish and heat through at 400°, about 15 minutes.

Stuffed Baked Tomatoes

(6 servings)

A handsome dish!

Wash and scoop out centers of

6 large tomatoes

Turn upside down to drain. Place in blender container

2 cups packed spinach
1 cup milk
3 tablespoons flour
3 tablespoons butter
½ cup diced cheese
½ teaspoon salt

Blend until spinach is coarsely chopped. Turn into saucepan and cook and stir until thick. Sprinkle tomatoes inside with

Salt and pepper

Fill with spinach mixture. Top with

½ cup soft bread crumbs (1 slice bread, blended)
¼ cup grated cheese

Bake in shallow pan at 350°, moderate oven, 15 minutes or until thoroughly hot.

Vegetable Nut Loaf

(8 servings)

Meatless, but "meaty"—a light, full-flavored loaf.

Blender-crumb, not too fine

> Sliced bread to make 1½ cups soft crumbs

Chop in blender and mix

> 1 cup walnuts
> ½ medium onion, cut in chunks
> 1½ cups cooked carrots

Add crumbs, also

> 3 slightly beaten eggs
> 1½ cups milk
> 1½ cups cooked or canned peas
> 1½ teaspoons salt
> ¼ teaspoon pepper
> 1½ tablespoons melted butter

Pack into well-greased loaf pan, about 9½ by 5½ inches. Bake at 350° for 1 hour. Serve with tomato or mushroom sauce.

Rice and Nut Loaf

(6 to 8 servings)

No meat, but it tastes like meat!

Place in blender container

> 1 8-ounce can tomato sauce
> 1 egg
> 1 rib celery with tops, cut in pieces
> 2 medium-sized onions, quartered
> 4 or 5 sprigs parsley
> 1 teaspoon salt
> ½ teaspoon sage
> 2 tablespoons butter or oil

Blend until vegetables are cut fine. Add and blend just a second or two

> 1 cup walnuts

Fold in

> 1½ cups cooked rice
> 1 cup cracker crumbs (can be prepared in blender)

Pour into greased loaf pan about 9½ by 5½ inches and bake at 350° for 1 hour. Serve with tomato sauce.

13 | Pantry Shelf Items

Almond Paste

(Well over a pint)

For roll and coffee-cake fillings and candies.

Place in blender container

> ½ cup orange juice
> 1 cup blanched almonds
> 1 cup sugar

Blend until nuts are very fine. Add

> 1 cup more almonds

Blend again until nuts are fine. Store this good paste in a covered jar in the refrigerator to use as you want it. For candy centers, work confectioners' sugar into it until it holds shape firmly, then dip in melted chocolate.

Good Peppery Chili Sauce

(4 pints)

You'll want to eat it all by itself!

Blender-chop, in small amounts, and place in preserving kettle

4 medium onions, quartered
1 small banana pepper, sliced
3 green peppers, cut in pieces
4 ribs celery, in inch slices

Add

6 pounds peeled tomatoes
1 cup vinegar
½ cup sugar
1 tablespoon salt
½ teaspoon cinnamon
½ teaspoon allspice

Cook gently for 1½ hours, or until mixture cooks down and thickens. Seal hot in canning jars.

Garden Relish

(6 pints)

You'll be proud to serve it with the roast.

Blender-chop, in small amounts with water (1½ quarts water, altogether), and empty into preserving kettle

1 medium head cauliflower, cut in chunks
3 cucumbers, pared, sliced thick
4 large onions, cut in eighths
3 cups celery, in 1-inch pieces
½ medium cabbage, cut in chunks
2 sweet red peppers, cut in pieces
1 green pepper, cut in pieces
1 hot pepper, cut in pieces

Add ⅓ cup salt, let stand overnight, then drain well. Prepare this sirup and boil 5 minutes

1 quart white vinegar
3 cups sugar
2 tablespoons each: mustard seed, celery seed
½ teaspoon turmeric

Add sirup to vegetables, bring to boil and simmer 15 minutes. Seal while hot in canning jars.

Golden Marmalade

(5 half-pints)

Color, flavor, consistency—all perfect!

Set aside in preserving kettle

> ½ pound dried apricots
> 1 cup water
> 1 can (9 ounces) pineapple tidbits, with juice

In blender container place

> ¼ cup water

Add and blend until chopped

> 1 orange, cut in pieces, seeds removed
> ½ lemon, cut in pieces, seeds removed

Add to fruit in kettle, with

> 2½ cups sugar
> 2 pounds peaches, chopped by hand
> 2 sticks cinnamon

Heat to boiling, lower heat and simmer gently for 1½ hours, or until thickened. Stir occasionally during cooking. Seal in clean hot canning jars.

Pepper Relish

(4 pints)

Green tomatoes, rather than red ones, are required.

Blender-chop in small amounts and turn into preserving kettle

> 3 red peppers, cut in pieces
> 3 green peppers, cut in pieces
> 3 large onions, cut in eighths
> 2 quarts quartered green tomatoes

Add
> 1 tablespoon each: celery seed, turmeric, mustard
> seed, salt
> 2 cups sugar
> 2 cups vinegar*

Bring to a boil, and cook for 45 minutes or until mixture thickens. Seal in clean hot jars.

* May be used to facilitate chopping vegetables.

Tomato Relish

(6 pints)

Easy and ever so delicious!

Blender-chop, in small amounts, and empty into preserving kettle
> 6 medium onions, quartered
> 6 large green apples, cored, sliced
> 3 green peppers, cut in pieces
> 3 red peppers, cut in pieces
> 6 peeled tomatoes, cut in quarters

Add
> 2½ cups sugar
> 2 cups vinegar*
> 1 tablespoon salt

Cook about 1½ hours or until thick, stirring occasionally. Seal in hot canning jars.

* May be used to facilitate chopping vegetables.

Cranberry Relish

(2 cups)

How versatile can you get?

Chop in blender, in small amounts
> 2 cups washed cranberries
> 1 whole orange, quartered, seeded

Stir in

> 1 cup sugar

Delightful and variable: You can add a blender-chopped apple or ½ cup blender-chopped nuts. Or ½ cup blender-chopped celery or 1 cup crushed pineapple. Or drain off liquid and add the relish to a package of lemon gelatin dissolved in 2 cups hot liquid which includes the drained juices. Chill and serve as salad.

Grated Coconut

It was always hard work to grate coconut until the advent of the blender. Now you crack the coconut, pick out the meat, pare off the brown part and do your grating in the blender. The process works faster if you cover blender blades with water, coconut water or milk (about ¼ cup), and of course it is important not to do too much at a time. If you want dry grated coconut for a cake, merely drain off the liquid after preparing it. You can toast the drained coconut in a moderate oven, if you like, but spread it out thin on a cooky sheet to do it most successfully.

Frozen or Canned Fruit Juices

The blender is ideal for reconstituting frozen fruit juice. Turn the orange juice or other frozen breakfast drink into the blender, add 2¼ cups water (or 3 cans full), cover and use low speed. Quick blending improves the flavor of canned citrus juices by aeration.

Index

Index